Is My *Faith* My Own?

A Resource for Christian Young People Leaving Home for the First Time

S. E. Thomas

Is My Faith My Own?
A Resource for Christian Young People Leaving
Home for the First Time

Published by The Dramatic Pen Press, L.L.C.
&
Life's Midterm Online Resources

Finding Hope Resource Guides
Volume One

Lolo, Montana

ISBN-10: 0692533850
ISBN-13: 978-0692533857

"I believe in Christianity as I believe that the sun has risen; not only because I see it, but because by it I see everything else."

~ C. S. LEWIS

For my children:
Yesenia, Dakota, and Novik

And for all my nieces and nephews:
Sarah, Micah, Hannah, Karah,
Jonathan, Violet, Alexander (Gus-Gus),
Josiah, Ethan, Caleb, Kahlan, and any who
might come after them.

ACKNOWLEDGEMENTS

My deepest thanks and appreciation to those who served as reviewers for this project, giving of their time and expertise to help make this book the best it could be:

Nathan Anglen
Youth Pastor, Bridge Bible Fellowship,
Moscow, ID

Dr. Rev. David Brown, Ed.D.
Pastor, Missionary to South and Central America, Christian Educator
Birmingham, AL

Rev. David Evans
Pastor, Salt River Baptist Church
Danville, KY

Rev. Jacob Gonzales
Pastor, Crosslands Bible Church
Thoreau, NM, Navajo Reservation

John Lipscomb
Anglican Lay Minister
Wales, United Kingdom

Berry Long
Campus Minister, InterVarsity Christian Fellowship
Gainesville, FL

Vicki Lucas, M.A.
Former Youth Minister, Christian Author
Missoula, MT

Adina McCloy
writer, Wycliffe Bible Translators
Missoula, MT

Rev. Joshua McNeal
Pastor, Mountain View Chapel
Twin Bridges, MT

Donna Miller
High School Teacher
College Station, TX

David Opitz
Missoula, MT

Eli Spire
Student Ministry Director, Missoula Alliance
Church
Missoula, MT

Ryan Sullivan
Student Ministry Director, Missoula Alliance
Church
Missoula, MT

Another Special Thanks To:
Laurie, Edd, Liwen, and Caryl

All Scripture was taken from the NIV.

TABLE OF CONTENTS

I
IT'S UP TO ME

Y ou think you have it all together. Then you get out on your own, and you realize it's your responsibility to get the rest of your life right.

What if you discover you were somehow misled in your faith in God?

It's still your responsibility to get that figured out.

If you're going to follow God, you must make that decision for yourself.

You can no longer coast by on your parents' faith, your pastor's understanding, or your youth leader's morals.

It's got to be yours.

And for it to be yours, you have to be sure you're right!

? ? ?

YIKES! Talk about a big deal!

But, before we dive in, let's get one thing straight. If you are feeling guilty for questioning your faith, don't. We all go through moments of searching as we grow and mature. It's a healthy part of learning and developing. If we never have questions, we'll never get the information we need to face the next challenge. Even worse, we run the risk of becoming ignorant and self-righteous.

In fact, the Bible tells us that the *only* reason you're able to be curious or interested in spiritual things in the first place is because *God Himself* is drawing you into a deeper relationship with Him or, maybe, into a brand new relationship with Him! That's exciting, too! John 6:44 says, *"No one can come to [Jesus] unless the Father who sent me draws him...."*

So, if you desire to know more about God and your place in the universe, that means *God Himself* is drawing you toward Himself... right now!

It's healthy to examine your faith from time to time to make sure you're on the right path. It's also healthy to seek out counsel from other believers who can provide some answers. Then compare what you are learning with what the Bible says (which you should do as often as possible). Acts 17:11 provides the following example, *"Now the Bereans were of more noble character than the Thessalonians, for they received the message with great eagerness and examined the Scriptures every day to see if what Paul said was true."*

So, you're doing just fine. You're doing exactly what Jesus wants you to do. The danger comes in when you seek the opinions of those who have no faith in God or the Bible to explain God or the Bible to you. For only by meeting God can you truly know Him. And the Bible itself is best suited to show you what it contains in its pages. After all, common sense tells us that, if you want to know about a thing, go straight to the source. (Because I firmly believe this, I have included many Bible passages within this guide.)

ONLY BY MEETING GOD CAN YOU TRULY KNOW HIM.

I'd like to introduce you to four people who have walked this path before:

Laurie was raised in a Christian home. Her mother was particularly strong in her faith, but in high school and college, Laurie made different choices. She says: "I decided I didn't want to go to church. It wasn't that I was rejecting God, I was just living my life and having fun. I didn't see the value or necessity of going to church every week."

Edd's father was in the military, so they bounced around between lots of different kinds of churches. Though Edd's parents made him go to church, they rarely attended themselves. As a young man, Edd found other ways to fill the voids in his life. He says, "I found the things that I felt gave me meaning among my friends, which was usually booze, girls, and cigarettes. Sex arrived in college. I made it through high school and 2 1/2 years of college before falling totally to Satan's lure."

Liwen's parents attended church, but that was the extent of their faith. When Liwen left home, she faced severe challenges within herself. She says, "When I went off to college, I was most challenged about being single and content, as compared to my friends/roommates who had found boyfriends. At one point I was the only person in our apartment of four who was not dating. This made me quite lonely and insecure."

Caryl was raised in a Christian home, but neither of her parents followed hard after God when she was young. Still, Caryl's desire was to follow the Lord. Caryl married her high school sweetheart, and they both attended church regularly. However, in the second year of her marriage, something happened at church, souring Caryl's opinion of it. "One of the other husbands in our couples' Sunday school class hit on me after some overt flirting. I ended up telling my husband about it. By year three, we went only sometimes… and not too often."

As you step out on your own, go to college, find a job, get married, you will face a number of challenges. That is a fact. There's no getting out of it or going around it. Bad things happen.

Jesus Himself gave this warning, *"In this world you will have trouble"* (John 16:33). Money will be scarce, things will break down, people will reject you and despise you, illnesses will interrupt your life, loved ones will die.

But Jesus did not give us that warning to depress us or rob us of our hope. Here's the full verse: *"I have told you these things, **so that in me you may have peace**. In this world you will have trouble. But take heart! I have overcome the world"* (emphasis added.)

Why did Jesus point out the coming troubles? To show us that *in Him* we could find peace. And how is that possible? Because He has overcome the world! This is incredibly good news!

So, let's continue our search. In order to attain the peace Jesus promises, you must first figure out if your faith is real. This book contains certain facts and evidence to help you recognize who Jesus is and understand His offer of salvation.

Once you know for sure you have a relationship with Jesus Christ, you must determine whether or not that relationship is growing. The last few chapters will walk you through the process of evaluating where you are before God and making decisions about where you need to go next.

By the end of your time spent in the pages of this book, it is my great hope that you will walk away with full knowledge of Jesus Christ, the joy of knowing you are eternally secure in Him, and basking in the peace He offers—no matter what troubles the world throws your way.

TALK IT OUT

1. What is the most exciting thing about being out on your own? The most frightening?

2. Can you identify with Lauri, Edd, Liwen, or Caryl? If so, how?

3. When it comes to your faith in God, how do you think it will fare over the next five years? Explain your response.

4. What evidence do you have that God is drawing you to Himself?

5. Where are you struggling in your faith right now? What gives you hope and security?

II
ASKING THE RIGHT QUESTIONS

L et me assure you of one thing. If you are asking the right questions, there are answers for all of them. But, what do I mean by 'asking the right questions?' Well, not all of our questions even make sense or are asked in the correct manner. Here are some examples of what I mean:

Some questions defy logic. For example: Can God make a boulder so large even He cannot lift it? Some people mistakenly believe that questions like this one somehow prove that God does not exist or, at best, is not all-powerful. They reason that, if God is all-powerful, He can do anything. But, if He can't make a boulder that large, He couldn't be all-powerful. If He *can* make a boulder that large but can't lift it, that, too, proves He is not all-powerful. So, if God is not all-powerful as the Bible claims, then the Bible is wrong. And if the Bible is wrong, then the God of the Bible may not even exist at all.

Of course, the above argument is complete foolishness. The question assumes that being *all-powerful* means *you can do anything*—even perform logical absurdities or go against your own nature. But that's not what power is, and the Bible never describes God that way. If we're talking about the God of the Bible (who created everything and then made mankind in His image), logic itself is part of His nature. And if logic is a part of God's nature, then it's not possible for God to step outside His nature and still be God. Furthermore, being all-powerful in no way demands that He is able to become that which He is not. (Even when God came to Earth as Jesus Christ—a man—He was still fully God or He could not have lived a sinless life, borne the sins of the world, nor conquered death.) Being all-powerful does not mean you can do anything. It means you, in your own nature and without any outside help, can do anything that requires power alone to do.

Some questions include the desired answer as a condition of the question itself. For example: Why does God allow bad things to happen to good people? Questions like these, in logic, succumb to the logical fallacy called 'begging the question.' This question explicitly assumes two things yet to be established: One, that God is "allowing" the evil in the world, and, two, that we are "good" people. Furthermore, the question implicitly assumes that, if God is good, then His good nature would prevent Him from allowing evil in any form to exist. So, the question itself is like asking a faithful, married man, "Why did you cheat on your wife?" The question assumes facts not in evidence and, in the same breath, makes an unfounded accusation. Only a guilty man could answer such a question. An innocent man could not.

Questions like these assume certain beliefs about God's nature to be true *before* any evidence has been examined. They skip a very important step in the quest for understanding. Better questions would be: "What are God's attributes? Is He 'good' and how can we tell? Does God allow bad things to happen? If so, why and for what purpose? Does the existence of evil in the world speak for or against the idea that God is good? Are human beings, in and of themselves, deserving of better treatment by God? If so, by what right do we cry foul? If not, how should we respond?" See the difference? The original question is an accusation and a demand. It is motivated by pride, not humility or a genuine longing to know God.

"WHEN PRIDE COMES, THEN COMES DISGRACE, BUT WITH HUMILITY COMES WISDOM."

PROVERBS 11:2

Some questions preemptively eliminate possible responses. For example: Is God male or female? Who's to say God must be either male or female? Questions like this also assume facts not in evidence and also fall prey to the 'begging the question' fallacy. This particular question assumes that God is limited in the same way humans are limited. A better question would be more open-ended, such as: What is God's nature? Or, is God gendered, genderless, or something else altogether? How is God described in the Bible?

There are a great many poorly conceived questions, and we cannot discuss them all here. However, the key thing to remember in posing a question is this:

When you ask a question about or of God, be sure the attitude with which you ask is one of humility, not one of pride. This is the correct attitude through which you will be able to understand God's answer when it comes.

Matthew 7:7-11 says, *"Ask and it will be given to you; seek and you will find; knock and the door will be opened to you. For everyone who asks receives; he who seeks finds; and to him who knocks, the door will be opened. Which of you, if his son asks for bread, will give him a stone? Or if he asks for a fish, will give him a snake? If you, then, though you are evil, know how to give good gifts to your children, how much more will your Father in heaven give good gifts to those who ask him!"*

"IF ANY OF YOU
LACKS WISDOM, HE
SHOULD ASK GOD,
WHO GIVES
GENEROUSLY TO
ALL WITHOUT
FINDING FAULT,
AND IT WILL BE
GIVEN TO HIM."

JAMES 1:5

TALK IT OUT

1. What, if any, question about God, Jesus, or the Bible have you struggled with? Is the question sound? If not, what would be a better question?

2. What key ingredient do we need when we approach God with our questions?

3. What is the promise in James 1:5? How might you claim this promise the next time you come up against a hard question?

III

RECOGNIZING THE RIGHT ANSWERS

erhaps the biggest mistake we make in seeking God (aside from approaching Him with pride rather than humility), is to fail to understand that not all questions require the same sort of answer. Typically, when I ask, "What does two plus two equal?" someone will answer, "Two plus two equals four." I asked a simple question and the correct answer came to me in the form of a simple statement. Given this victory, I might be tempted to assume that all questions, if posed as a simple question, should be answerable in a similar way—with just a statement of fact. But I would be severely mistaken.

Some answers come in a very different form than the question itself. Consider the question: How do I ride a bike?

It sounds like a simple question, but no simple statement in response will do. Even if I were to respond with an entire expository on the invention and mechanical processes of bicycles, the required motions of the muscles and ligaments involved in riding bicycles, and the physics of staying upright while in motion, the inquirer would not have received the desired information which motivated the question. She would not be any more able to ride a bike than she was prior to asking the question. Because, in this case, the knowledge sought is not knowledge of a fact, but knowledge of a skill. Her knowledge of a skill (procedural knowledge) is very different than the knowing of a fact (propositional knowledge.) No mere statement will satisfy such a question. The inquirer must experience repeated practice on an actual bicycle—in effect, living out the 'answer'—before being able to claim that knowledge.

Here's another example: What is love?

Can this question be answered with a statement of fact? I might respond with: Love is choosing the highest good for the other person. But, as accurate as that description might be, it does not convey the 'what it is like' to be loved. For this depth of understanding, the inquirer must actually *experience* being loved and loving another. Aside from the experience itself, the answer will make little sense to the inquirer.

SOME ANSWERS COME IN A DIFFERENT FORM THAN THE QUESTION ITSELF.

Some questions must be answered, not with a statement, but with an experience. Here, too, the inquirer must live out the answer—in this case, the necessary relationship—that corresponds to this question.

So, as we proceed, keep in mind that not all of the answers you seek will come in the form of simple

SOME TRUTHS MUST BE *LIVED* TO BE UNDERSTOOD.

statements of fact, true or false, yes or no. Not all information or knowledge is of that variety. Some things go way deeper and take more time. Some truths must be *lived* to be understood.

TALK IT OUT

1. What kind of knowledge can be acquired and transferred via a simple statement?

2. What are some kinds of knowledge that must be lived out or experienced to be acquired or understood?

3. Discuss some ways getting to know a person (a being) is different from having a belief.

IV
HOW CAN I KNOW GOD IS REAL?

P eople struggle with this question a lot, but that's no reason you have to. The answer to this question is actually pretty simple. We can know God is real because we are here and, frankly, the only other alternative is severely flawed.

Atheism claims that science is an infallible source of truth and knowledge about the world but, in the same breath, wants you to believe the universe created itself out of nothing and that intelligent life sprang (again, by itself) out of non-living matter. But we know that is utter foolishness, because it contradicts the tenets of science and reality.

Given the laws of physics, there is absolutely no known (or even intelligently imagined) mechanism by which even the tiniest speck of matter in the universe could possibly exist without an intelligent and all-powerful force making it. We can't even conceive of such a thing. So we know God must exist. Yet atheism demands that you accept at face value something they have not even begun to explain[1],

---

[1] This is not to say that no atheist has ever *attempted* an explanation. Some attempts have been made; however, they are so very poor, and they so deeply defy reason or logic, they cannot possibly be correctly labeled true

let alone defend, and which contradicts every other commitment they make in their quest for truth. Talk about checking your brain in at the door.

No. There has to be a God who created everything. And, if He created everything, His creation will be a reflection of Him, not a denial of Him.

SCIENCE HAS AS MUCH TO TEACH US ABOUT GOD AS ANYTHING ELSE.

Science, therefore, has as much to teach us about God as anything else. We have absolutely nothing to fear from science—only a great deal to learn. In fact, the Bible says, *"The heavens declare the glory of God; the skies proclaim the work of his hands"* (Psalm 19:1).

As it happens, science has already taught us some pretty amazing things about God and His design of us. Here are a few:

"explanations." An explanation should, I believe, be capable of, at least, being conceived of. I have to be able to see some kind of rationality within it that matches known reality. Sadly (inevitably?), their attempts fail every time. For example, Stephen Hawking suggests something called "imaginary time," but even he admits it is only a metaphysical idea and says that, in real time, the universe has a beginning. (Stephen W. Hawking, *A Brief History of* Time (New York: Bantam, 1988), 136-139.)

1. According to the Principle of Uniformity, past causes are like the causes we observe today. In other words, we can assume the world works pretty much the same today as it has in the past—particularly when it comes to causes. That means that if we observe today that intelligent life can only come from previous intelligent life (which we do), then this has always been so. That means that the first living matter had to come from living matter and that the first intelligent life could only have come from other intelligent life. This points to an Intelligent Designer.

2. Darwin's assumption that life could have sprung from non-living matter (on its own) was dependent on his belief that the first life was incredibly simple. However, even the simplest form of life requires DNA—a highly specific and orderly set of chemicals which spell out a detailed and unique genetic message. The DNA of a one-celled amoeba, if spelled out in chemical sequence, would fill 1,000 encyclopedias. There is no such thing as "simple" life.

3. Atheists and Darwinists claim that, if given enough time, everything in existence today would come about

through random chance. However, the Second Law of Thermodynamics, in part, states that entropy (disorder) increases with time.

4. In order for life to exist on Earth, over 100 fine-tuned physical constants are required. (More on this in the next chapter.)

Paul says, in Romans 1:20, *"For since the creation of the world God's invisible qualities— his eternal power and divine nature—have been clearly seen, being understood from what has been made, so that men are without excuse."*

Another way to know God is real is by recognizing the nature of morality. The Darwinist worldview emphasizes survival of the fittest—the strong usurping or even eliminating the weak. But moral law tells us that this kind of attitude is wrong. We are supposed to help those who are weaker and be kind and patient with one another. We are supposed to work together, never leaving anyone behind. But why? If biology and mankind as a species is benefitted by removing the weak and infirm from among us, why should we feel any compassion at all for anyone weaker than ourselves?

If we were to look up the word "morality" in a dictionary, we would find it defined as rules governing right and wrong. But the words "rules" and "right" and "wrong" make zero sense outside of relationship. Morality is about how people treat other people. Furthermore, because morality is an overarching code to which we all ascribe and are accountable, it can only be fully understood within the context of a relationship with a Being greater than us. Let me explain:

People are inherently flawed and easily deceived. Everything we know, we learn from those who came before us, including moral imperatives. A single individual is incapable of creating his or her own moral law, apart from input from others, because moral law is *about* our relationships with others. Moral law makes no sense for the individual since there is no one to be right or wrong to. So, morality cannot come from the individual.

Communities and nations do exist within a framework of relationship. In order to achieve our goals, we must work together, which requires following certain aspects of moral law. However, there is a great deal of disagreement, between nations (and amongst ourselves), regarding what is right and what is wrong. Some people groups send their elderly off to die alone, others believe the young are obligated to care for their parents and grandparents in their old age. Some nations embrace forced abortion to deal with a perceived population problem, other nations believe such a thing is a violation of female and human rights. Some communities practice female mutilation; others reject it as a gross human rights violation. Some nations embrace torturing and/or killing those who don't profess a particular faith; other nations believe in the freedom of religion.

Though there is a great deal of disagreement between societies regarding morality, we know *there is a higher standard that governs them all—because all human beings must be of equal, inherent worth.* If it's wrong in one society to abandon one's grandmother, then it's wrong for all grandmothers to be abandoned. If it's wrong to mutilate a white, American 13-year-old girl's genitals, then it's wrong to mutilate a black, African little girl's genitals.

> WE KNOW THERE IS A HIGHER STANDARD THAT GOVERNS ALL MORAL LAW—BECAUSE ALL HUMAN BEINGS ARE OF EQUAL, INHERENT WORTH.

Evil cannot be reasonably or satisfactorily justified based on the reasoning: "Well, it's just what those people do." Such flippant lack of consideration for others must be rejected on the basis that the innocent little girl who is being tortured is just as valuable and precious as our own little girls and little sisters. To abandon children to such treatment and to allow foolishness or selfishness or evil to reign unchecked is abhorrent. Such inconsiderate attitudes create a very slippery slope toward a general disregard for human life at every level—for if we can justify the torture or abandonment of one human being, we can justify it for all.

> IF WE CAN JUSTIFY THE
> TORTURE OR
> ABANDONMENT OF ONE
> HUMAN BEING, WE CAN
> JUSTIFY IT FOR ALL.

No reasonable, objective standard exists for making it okay to torture one child over another—therefore, all human beings are of equal, inherent worth. Furthermore, the fact that humanity cannot agree on a definition of basic, humane treatment of one another, shows that morality does not come from human agreements arising from groups or communities of people.

So, here is a moral argument for God's existence (four premises/reasons and a conclusion):

1. Moral law exists.
2. Morality does not arise from the individual.
3. Morality does not arise from groups of people (communities, nations, etc.)
4. The only other possible source of morality is God.

C. ***Therefore, morality must come from God. God exists.***

God's existence is demanded by the fact that an objective standard of morality exists: the equal, inherent value of all mankind and the demand to treat one another accordingly. Because this imperative cannot possibly have come from us, and the only other logical source is a higher, intelligent, and moral source, God must exist. (And not only does He exist, but He is *good*.)

Though much more could be said on this subject, I am going to end here. But, just for good measure, let's listen to a voice from the world of science. Robert Jastrow, an astronomer who served as the director of Mount Wilson and founded NASA's Goddard Institute of Space Studies, is an agnostic, but even he can't deny the evidence. He said, "Astronomers now find they have painted themselves into a corner because they have proven, by their own methods, that the world began abruptly in an act of creation to which you can trace the seeds of every star, every planet, every living thing in this cosmos and on the earth. And they have found that all of this happened as a product of forces they cannot hope to discover.... *That there are what I or anyone would call supernatural forces at work is now, I think, a scientifically proven fact.*"[2]

We know God is real because He must be real. We know God is real because there are no scientifically, morally, spiritually, intellectually, or relationally sound alternatives.

TALK IT OUT

1. Is science the enemy of faith in God? Why or why not?

2. How does God use His creation (i.e. scientific observation and discovery) to reveal Himself to us?

3. What might life be like in the absence of moral law?

4. How does the existence morality prove God's existence and His goodness?

5. What are some scientific questions about God's existence that you would like answered?

---

[2] "A Scientist Caught Between Two Faiths: Interview with Robert Jastrow," *Christianity Today*, August 6, 1982, emphasis added.

V

HOW CAN I KNOW GOD CARES ABOUT ME?

K nowing God exists and knowing God is a personal being who cares about you are two different concepts, but they are related and, as it happens, the same evidence that shows us the one thing also shows us the other. We know God exists because a lot of other stuff exists, and it couldn't have gotten here on its own. But we know God cares about us in a loving, personal way because of the *way* He created everything, including us.

If God was an impersonal force, it is unlikely intelligent life would exist at all. Just as living matter cannot spring from non-living matter, intelligent properties cannot and do not arise from non-intelligent properties. At no time in all of recorded history has such a thing been known to have happened. Furthermore, if God didn't really care about us in every single detail, why did He bother paying so much attention to the details that would make our lives possible?

In their book, "I Don't Have Enough Faith to Be an Atheist," Drs. Norman Geisler and Frank Turek recorded fifteen incredible ways (though there are, in fact, hundreds) God uniquely tuned our universe to support life. I include them here:

1. The oxygen level on earth comprises 21 percent of the atmosphere, making life on earth possible. If oxygen were 25 percent, fires would erupt spontaneously; if it were 15 percent, we would suffocate.

2. If the atmosphere were less transparent, not enough solar radiation would reach the world's surface to sustain life. If it were more transparent, we would be poisoned by too much solar radiation.

3. If the moon-Earth gravitational interaction was greater than it currently is, tidal effects on the oceans, atmosphere, and rotational period would be too severe. If it were less, orbital changes would cause climactic instabilities.

4. If the CO_2 level were higher, a runaway greenhouse effect would develop, causing us to all burn up. If it were lower, plants would not be able to maintain efficient photosynthesis, and we would suffocate.

5. If the gravitational force were altered by 0.0000000000000000000000000000000000001 percent, our sun would not exist and, therefore, neither would we.

6. If the centrifugal force of planetary movements did not precisely balance the gravitational forces, nothing could be held in orbit around the sun.

7. If the universe had expanded at a rate one millionth more slowly than it did, expansion would have stopped, and the universe would have collapsed on itself before any stars had formed. If it had expanded faster, no galaxies would have formed.

8. Any of the laws of physics can be described as a function of the velocity of light (now defined to be 299,792,458 meters per second). Even a slight variation in the speed of light would alter the other constants and make life on earth impossible.

9. If water vapor levels in the atmosphere were greater than they are, a runaway greenhouse effect would cause temperatures to rise too high for human life; if they were less, an insufficient greenhouse effect would make the earth too cold to support life.

10. Jupiter's current orbit prevents the earth from being bombarded with space material. Jupiter's gravitational field acts

as a cosmic vacuum cleaner, attracting asteroids and comets that might otherwise strike earth.

11. If the thickness of the earth's crust were greater, too much oxygen would be transferred to the crust to support life. If it were thinner, volcanic and tectonic activity would make life impossible.

12. If the rotation of the earth took longer than 24 hours, temperature differences would be too great between night and day. If the rotation period were shorter, atmospheric wind velocities would be too great.

13. The 23-degree axil tilt of the earth is just right. If the tilt were altered slightly, surface temperatures would be too extreme on earth.

14. If the atmospheric discharge (lightning) rate were greater, there would be too much fire destruction; if it were less, there would be too little nitrogen in the soil.

15. If there were more seismic activity, much more life would be lost; if there was less, nutrients on the ocean floors and in river runoff would not be cycled

back to the continents through tectonic uplift.

God had you in mind from the very beginning. He made this beautiful, finely-tuned world that, in every detail, reflects its Creator, and then He gave it to you—not just so you would have something awesome, but so you could see *Him* in it. But the universe was not the only thing He fine-tuned. He took extra special care to create you, as well—every part for a specific purpose.

FOR YOU CREATED MY INMOST BEING; YOU KNIT ME TOGETHER IN MY MOTHER'S WOMB. I PRAISE YOU BECAUSE I AM FEARFULLY AND WONDERFULLY MADE; YOUR WORKS ARE WONDERFUL, I KNOW THAT FULL WELL.

PSALM 139:13-14

The Bible tells us, *"Are not five sparrows sold for two pennies? Yet not one of them is forgotten by God. Indeed, the very hairs of your head are all numbered. Don't be afraid; you are worth more than many sparrows"* (Luke 12:6-

7). Jeremiah 31:3 says, *"I have loved you with an everlasting love; I have drawn you with loving-kindness."* But most of all, we know God cares about us through what He did on our behalf when He came as Jesus Christ. *"But God shows his love for us in that while we were still sinners, Christ died for us"* (Romans 5:8).

TALK IT OUT

1. If an impersonal force had been responsible for creation, how might the universe be different?

2. What are some ways God shows His love for mankind?

3. According to John 15:13, what is the greatest love of all? How does Jesus's love measure up? How does your love for Jesus measure up to this standard?

VI

HOW CAN I KNOW JESUS IS GOD? PART I

O f all the questions this book asks, this is the most vital. If we don't get this one right, nothing else we believe or do will matter. Lots of people believe in God, but live their lives alone, in fear, and facing a bleak future. Many of the people you know go to church, give to the needy, and talk passionately about various social issues, but are empty inside.

Jesus said, *"I am the way and the truth and the life. No one comes to the Father except through me"* (John 14:6).

If He was right, then it is vitally important that that we get to know Him—the real Jesus— not just the concept people toss around, the name people use to curse with, or the guy religious people talk about when they're trying to look pious.

If Jesus is an actual Being and not just a benign belief, and if He's the *only* way to get to God, then our **JESUS IS A *BEING* NOT A *BELIEF*.** understanding of who He is and our position in relation to Him will mean the difference between salvation and slavery, hope and despair, life and death, Heaven and Hell.

Because this question is so important, the following subsections cover EIGHT areas of evidence for you to examine so you can decide for yourself what you believe about Jesus Christ. Because there are so many, I will only deal with four at a time, but here they all are, in the order they will be presented:

1. *The Reliability of Scriptural Testimony*
2. *Jesus in the Context of History*
3. *Jesus and Fulfilled Prophesy*
4. *Jesus's Sinless Life*
5. *Jesus's Claim to be God*
6. *Jesus's Miracles*
7. *Jesus's Victory over Death*
8. *Jesus Among Other Gods*

1. *The Reliability of Scriptural Testimony*

There are certain facts that have been firmly established and are nearly universally recognized. One is that the Jesus of the Bible really and truly existed (which we will address in a moment). Another is that the Bible passages that tell of His life, death and resurrection were in circulation within the lifetimes of the people who knew Him.

The exact same Scriptures they had then say precisely what our modern Bibles say now. Thanks to the discovery of the Dead Sea Scrolls in 1947, we know the texts are the same.

But why is that so important? How does that help us determine that Scriptural testimony is both accurate and reliable?

Two reasons:

1. We know the passages haven't been altered to make us think stuff happened that really didn't. (So, they are accurate.)

2. Because we know what the writers and their audiences said and didn't say, they become incredibly reliable witnesses to the truth of what they saw, experienced, and believed. (So, they are reliable.)

We have in our hot little hands the very same words Jesus's friends and family members and followers had in theirs. That means nobody—not the disciples, not the church, not the scribes or copiers—changed anything in nearly 2,000 years of copying and passing them along. We know what they knew. We can read for ourselves exactly what they were reading. And, because the people of the day were reading it and knew Jesus and His followers personally, they are our *very best witnesses* to the authenticity of the Biblical accounts!

In fact, the New Testament writers were not only eyewitnesses themselves (2 Peter 1:16), but they also mentioned more than thirty names of people *who were alive at the time.*

Many of the names the New Testament writers mention are of very prominent people, such as Pilate, High Priest Caiaphas, Festus, and the entire Herodian family (Matthew 26-27, Mark 6:14-29, Acts 26). There is no way the New Testament writers could have spread a pack of lies intended to deceive, referenced such influential people (who hated them) to implicate them in fabricated events, passed these writings around a city in religious and political turmoil, and gotten away with it. Surely, someone would have called them out as liars, proven the stories false, and let the crazy ravings of a few die away naturally.

But that's not what happened. There were so many eye-witnesses to the resurrection still living that the fact of Jesus's resurrection was practically common knowledge. Over 500 people had seen the risen Christ with their own eyes after He had been crucified (I Corinthians 15), and a great many more witnessed the miracles being performed in His name. Most of these people were *still alive* at the time this letter was in circulation. So, the only thing the Romans and Jewish religious leaders could do was try to cover it up as best they could and persecute those who insisted on talking about it.

But even they could not deny the truth of Jesus Christ's victory over death. The evidence was simply too great. (We'll look at this evidence in more detail in a moment.)

2. Jesus in the Context of History

I may have already given you the best evidence for the historical existence of Jesus of Nazareth—the Scriptural, eyewitness testimony and the fact that we have the exact same documents in our hands that they had in theirs. It would be unthinkable that such documents with such detailed and amazing facts about a particular man could have been in circulation in that place and at the time without somebody somewhere saying, "Um… there's no such person as Jesus of Nazareth" if, in fact, He did not exist and, indeed, wasn't well known.

However, there is even more evidence for the historical existence of a real person named Jesus, the son of Joseph and Mary, who was born in Bethlehem, grew up in Nazareth, and died on a Roman cross on a hill called Golgotha just outside Jerusalem. Here are a few samples of this evidence: [3]

---

[3] For more, go to:
http://www.biblicalarchaeology.org/daily/people-cultures-in-the-bible/jesus-historical-jesus/did-jesus-exist/

1. Roman senator, orator, ethnographer, and historian, Cornelius Tacitus, (55/56-c. 118 C.E.) confirms, not only the historical existence of Jesus, but also the way He died. In Tacitus's work, *Annals*, written c. 116-117 C.E., he mentions Christians (whom he despised) stating, *"...whom the crowd called 'Chrestians.' The founder of this name, Christ, had been executed in the reign of Tiberius by the procurator Pontius Pilate."*

2. Flavius Josephus, a Jewish priest and historian, who lived in Rome 37-c. 100 C.E., corroborates the historical existence of Jesus and establishes His relationship to His brother James, the leader of the Christian church in Jerusalem. This reference is in Book 20 of Josephus's book, *Jewish Antiquities*: *"...the brother of Jesus-who-is-called-Messiah ...James by name...."* Because many others named Jesus also existed, Josephus clarifies which one he is referencing here ("Jesus-who-is-called-Messiah"), which would make no sense for him to do had the Jesus of the Bible not existed and been recognized by many as the Messiah. However, Josephus himself was not a Christian, as best as can be determined.

3. Flavius Josephus provides further evidence of the historical existence of Jesus in Book 18 of *Jewish Antiquities*, in a section known as the *Testimonium Flavianum*: "*Around this time there lived Jesus, a wise man, if indeed one ought to call him a man. For he was one who did surprising deeds, and a teacher of such people as accept the truth gladly. He won over many Jews and many of the Greeks. He was the Messiah. When Pilate, upon hearing him accused by men of the highest standing among us, had condemned him to be crucified, those who in the first place came to love him did not give up their affection for him, for on the third day, he appeared to them restored to life. The prophets of God had prophesied this and countless other marvelous things about him. And the tribe of Christians, so called after him, have still to this day not died out.*" Though some suspect this section may have been partially altered by Christian scribes, it still seems clear that, given the date it was written and its audience, it still serves as relatively good evidence for the historical existence of Jesus Christ of Nazareth.

4. Lucian of Samosata (c. 115-200 C.E.), a Greek satirist, clearly references Jesus in

two passages, albeit with contempt and sarcasm. I include one of them here: *"It was then that he learned the marvelous wisdom of the Christians, by associating with their priests and scribes in Palestine. And—what else?—in short order he made them look like children, for he was a prophet, cult leader, head of the congregation and everything, all by himself. He interpreted and explained some of their books, and wrote many himself. They revered him as a god, used him as a lawgiver, and set him down as a protector—to be sure, after that other whom they still worship, the man who was crucified in Palestine because he introduced this new cult into the world"* (*Passing of Peregrinus*, §11, as translated in Evans, "Jesus in Non-Christian Sources," p. 462).

5. Celsus, a Platonist philosopher, c. 176 C.E., considered Jesus to be a magician who made exorbitant claims: *"Next he makes the charge of the savior that it was by magic that he was able to do the miracles which he appeared to have done, and foreseeing that others also, having learned the same lessons and being haughty to act with the power of God, are about to do the same thing, such persons Jesus would drive away from his own society"* (Origen, *Against*

Celsus, 1.6, 38, as translated in Evans, "Jesus in Non-Christian Sources," p. 460).

6. Pliny the Younger, a Roman governor and friend of Tacitus, wrote about early Christian worship of Christ *"as to a god"* (Evans, "Jesus in Non-Christian Sources," p. 459).

7. As far as we know today, no ancient person ever argued that Jesus did not exist. *"The non-Christian testimonies to Jesus ...show that contemporaries in the first and second century saw no reason to doubt Jesus' existence"* (Theissen and Merz, *Historical Jesus*, p. 63). Robert Van Voorst observes, *"[N]o pagans and Jews who opposed Christianity denied Jesus' historicity or even questioned it"* (*Jesus Outside*, p. 15). Van Voorst goes on to say, *"[I]f anyone in the ancient world had a reason to dislike the Christian faith, it was the rabbis. To argue successfully that Jesus never existed but was a creation of early Christians would have been the most effective polemic against Christianity ...[Yet] all Jewish sources treated Jesus as a fully historical person ...[T]he rabbis ...used the real events of Jesus'*

life against him" (*Jesus Outside*, pg. 133-134).

Other extra-biblical evidences exist, as well, such as writings by Suetonius (a Roman writer, lawyer, and historian), a letter from Mara Bar Serapion to his son describing "the wise Jewish king," and various archeological finds; however, I have run out of space here to discuss them all. Suffice it to say, the evidence for the existence of Jesus Christ within the context of known history is extensive, and most serious scholars do not deny the fact.

3. *Jesus and Fulfilled Prophesy*

It is estimated that there are approximately 300 prophesies recorded in the Bible about the Messiah—everything from what family He would be born into to what kind of life He would live to how He would die. There are even some about what He would do *after* He died—such as coming back to life under His own power and then coming back a second time to conquer sin once and for all, judge all people, and create a new earth where those who believed in Him would live together in harmony in His presence. Most of these prophesies have been fulfilled down to some incredibly precise details, but we're still waiting for a few—such as those relating to Jesus's second coming.

While we still have to wait for those final ones to happen, all those which chronologically precede Christ's second coming can be examined for accuracy—and they are *100 percent* accurate.

In fact, the New Testament writers who recorded these events actually challenged their readers to deny that what they said was true: *"Fellow Israelites, listen to this: Jesus of Nazareth was a man accredited by God to you by miracles, wonders and signs, which God did **among you** through him, **as you yourselves know"*** (Acts 2:22) (emphasis added).

I don't have time here to go over all of the prophesies Jesus fulfilled, but I will share several with you which, I feel, speak volumes about Jesus's divinity—for only someone with God's power, timelessness, and insights could have pulled them off:

1. The fact that the Messiah would be born in Bethlehem was prophesied in Micah 5:2, written c. 750-700 B.C.E.: *"But you, Bethlehem Ephrathah, though you are small among the clans of Judah, out of you will come for me one who will be ruler over Israel, whose origins are from of old, from ancient times."* Jesus fulfilled this prophesy (Matthew 2:1 & Luke 2:4-6).

2. At least two prophesies exist that stated that the Messiah would be an heir to King David's throne: 2 Samuel 7:12-13 and Isaiah 9:7. Jesus of Nazareth fulfills this requirement, as recorded in Luke 1:32-33 and Romans 1:3.

3. The prophet Jeremiah prophesied that a massacre of children would happen at the Messiah's birthplace: *"A voice is heard in Ramah, mourning and great weeping, Rachel weeping for her children and refusing to be comforted, because they are no more"* (Jeremiah 31:15). This sorrowful prophesy was fulfilled when Herod the Great slaughtered the children of Bethlehem in his power-hungry desire to secure his reign from any who might threaten it (Matthew 2:16-18).

4. The prophet Isaiah wrote, *"Therefore the Lord himself will give you a sign: The virgin will conceive and give birth to a son, and will call him Immanuel,"* prophesying that the Messiah would be born of a virgin and be called Immanuel. Jesus fulfilled both of these prophesies (Matthew 1:22-23 & Luke 1:26-31).

5. Both Psalm 41:9 and Zechariah 11:12-13 prophesy that the Messiah would be betrayed, which is what Judas did to

Jesus, as recorded in Luke 22:47-48 and Matthew 26:14-16.

6. After the crucifixion of Jesus Christ, the chief priests used the thirty silver coins (which they had paid Judas for betraying Jesus and which he had later thrown at their feet) to purchase a field belonging to a local potter (Matthew 27:3-7). This event was prophesied (directly orchestrated by God, in fact) in an event between God and the prophet Zechariah over 500 years earlier. *"I told them, 'If you think it best, give me my pay; but if not, keep it.' So they paid me thirty pieces of silver. And the LORD said to me, 'Throw it to the potter'—the handsome price at which they priced me! So I took the thirty pieces of silver and threw them into the house of the LORD to the potter"* (Zechariah 11:12-13).

7. In John 19:23. It says, *"When the soldiers crucified Jesus, they took his clothes, dividing them into four shares, one for each of them, with the undergarment remaining. This garment was seamless, woven in one piece from top to bottom."* This event was prophesied by King David in Psalm 22:17-18. It reads, *"I can count all my bones; people stare and gloat over me.*

They divide my garments among them and cast lots for my clothing."

Such events as these could not have been orchestrated by an ordinary man (nor would an ordinary man want to even try). There are *hundreds* of prophesies like these that Jesus fulfilled. [4]

4. Jesus's Sinless Life

There are two lines of evidence we can reference here to show that Jesus did, indeed, live a sinless life. One is the testimony of those who knew Him. The other is the lack of evidence that He ever sinned. Since we cannot list that which does not exist, we will focus on the former; however, I will note that Jesus was crucified for blasphemy—that is to say, He was accused and convicted of claiming to be God—which would be a sin unless, of course, He was God. By the end of this discussion, I believe you'll agree that the evidence fully supports His claim. Therefore, below I will outline the testimonial evidence in support of Jesus having lived an entire life free from sin:

1. *"He committed no sin, and no deceit was found in his mouth"* (I Peter 2:22).

---

[4] For a list of 44 fulfilled prophesies, go to:
http://christianity.about.com/od/biblefactsandlists/a/Prophecies-Jesus.htm

2. *"And in him is no sin"* (I John 3:5b).

3. Jesus himself said, *"Can any of you prove me guilty of sin"* (John 8:46a)?

4. The prophet Isaiah prophesied that the Messiah would be without sin: *"He was assigned a grave with the wicked, and with the rich in his death, though he had done no violence, nor was any deceit in his mouth"* (Isaiah 53:9).

5. Pontius Pilate found no reason to crucify Jesus, saying, *"I find no basis for a charge against this man"* (Luke 23:4).

6. The thief who hung next to Jesus said, *"We are punished justly, for we are getting what our deeds deserve. But this man has done nothing wrong"* (Luke 23:41).

7. Jesus was tempted by Satan in Luke 4, but resisted. Hebrews 4:15 states, *"For we do not have a high priest who is unable to empathize with our weaknesses, but we have one who has been tempted in every way, just as we are—yet he did not sin."*

8. Jesus repeatedly found solitary places to pray and seek help from God to avoid

temptation (Luke 6:12, Matthew 14:23, Mark 1:35, John 17).

9. Only a sinless sacrifice is worthy of taking on the sins of the world. I Peter 2:24 explains, *"'He himself bore our sins' in his body on the cross, so that we might die to sins and live for righteousness; 'by his wounds you have been healed.'"*

TALK IT OUT

1. What evidence do you have that shows Scriptural testimony about Jesus Christ to be both accurate and reliable?

2. Why is it important that we have extra-biblical corroboration for what the Bible says about the historical Jesus?

3. What does Jesus's fulfillment of the ancient prophesies about the Messiah tell us?

4. Why is it important to know that Jesus lived a sinless life?

VII
How Can I Know Jesus is God? Part II

T hough the last chapter contains a great deal of evidence for Jesus being God, we aren't even close to covering it all. And keep in mind that, even with everything I present here, I'm really only grazing the surface of all that is available in Scripture, archaeology, and the historical record. I deeply encourage you to do some digging for yourself. But, for now, let's jump right back in where we left off:

5. *Jesus's Claim to be God*

Jesus claimed to be God—not just *a god* but *the God*, the Creator of all things, including you and me. In fact, that's the reason the Jewish leaders had Him crucified. But Jesus did more than claim to be God. He behaved in a way as to back it up. Though the following is not an exhaustive list of these events, the main details are provided below:

1. *Things Jesus Said:*
   a. He called God His Father, making Himself equal with God. (John 5:18)
   b. He referred to Himself as "I am," which is a reference to the name God

gave Himself in Exodus 3:14. (John 8:58)

c. He was nearly stoned for claiming, *"I and the Father are one,"* (John 10:30-33).

d. He was condemned for blasphemy when He claimed to be the Messiah before the high priest, referencing the Exodus 3:14 passage again and claiming to be the fulfillment of Daniel 7:13-14, which is a prophesy of the coming Messiah (Mark 14:61-64).

2. *Jesus Showed Himself to be All-Knowing.*
   a. He predicted that Peter would disown Him three times before the rooter crowed. (Matthew 26:34)
   b. He predicted His own death and resurrection on the third day. (Matthew 26:21 & Mark 9:31)
   c. He predicted that the disciples would fall away for a time. (Matthew 26:31)

3. *Jesus Showed Himself to be All-Powerful.*
   a. His miracles
   b. His fulfillment of prophesy
   c. His resurrection

4. ***Jesus Claimed Omnipresence*** (being everywhere at all times).

a. He promised to *always* be with His disciples. (Matthew 28:20)

b. Three times, He referred to Himself as the Alpha and the Omega in John's prophetic visions. (Revelation 1:8, 21:6, 22:13)

c. He was chosen as our perfect sacrifice before the creation of the world. (I Peter 1:18-20)

5. ***Jesus Claimed the Authority to Forgive Sins.***

a. He forgave a paralyzed man. (Mark 2:9 & Luke 5:20)

b. He forgave a sinful woman. (Luke 7:36-50)

6. ***Jesus Accepted Worship as God.***

a. As a small child He was worshipped by the magi. (Matthew 2:11)

b. He welcomed worship as the long-awaited Messiah when He fulfills prophesy by entering Jerusalem riding on a foal. (Matthew 21:9 & John 12:13)

c. He accepted His disciples' worship after they saw Him walk on water. (Matthew 14:33)

    d. He accepted the worship of His female disciples after His resurrection. (Matthew 28:9)

    e. He accepted Thomas's worship after His resurrection. (John 20:28)

7. ***Jesus Became the Sinless and Perfect Sacrifice in our Place.***

    a. He was tempted, but did not sin. (Hebrews 4:15)

    b. He is called the perfect high priest. (Hebrews 7:26-28)

    c. He is called the perfect sacrifice, worthy to take our place. (Hebrews 10:1-18, II Corinthians 5:21, John 3:5, I Peter 1:18-19 & 2:22)

8. ***Jesus's Transfiguration of Mark 9:1-8.***

    a. He changed before their eyes into the figure of God (v. 3).

    b. He summoned and spoke with Elijah and Moses, who had been dead for centuries (v. 4).

    c. God Himself spoke audibly from Heaven declaring Jesus as His Son (v. 7).

9. ***Jesus's Baptism of Matthew 3:13-17.***

    a. The Holy Spirit descended from Heaven and alighted on Jesus "as a dove" (v. 16).

b. God Himself spoke audibly from Heaven declaring Jesus as His Son (v. 17).

6. *Jesus's Miracles*

If one does not count the hundreds of prophesies Jesus fulfilled, His supernatural ability to read the minds and experiences of other people, and His ability to foretell future events (all which seem pretty miraculous to me), Jesus performed at least 40 other miracles, including His own resurrection. Here I categorize them as to type—each important to establish His fullness as God incarnate. I also include two sections with only a few examples of the many times Jesus demonstrated supernatural knowledge.

1. *Jesus Exercised Power over Disease & Human Deformity.* (Matthew 8:1-4, 8:5-13, 8:14-15, 8:16-17, 9:1-8, 9:20-22, 9:27-31, 9:32-34, 12:9-14, 14:34-36, 20:29-34, Mark 7:31-37, 8:22-26, Luke 13:10-17, 14:1-6, 17:11-19, 22:50-51, John 4:43-53, 5:1-15, 9:1-12)

2. *Jesus Exercised Power over Animals.* (Matthew 17:24-27, Luke 5:1-11, John 21:4-11)

3. *Jesus Exercised Power over Plants.*
(Matthew 21:18-22)

4. *Jesus Exercised Power over Death.*
(Matthew 9:18-26, 28, Luke 7:11-17,
John 11:1-45)

5. *Jesus Exercised Power over Natural
Elements.* (Matthew 14:13-21, 14:22-33,
15:32-39, John 2:1-11)

6. *Jesus Exercised Power over the
Weather.* (Matthew 8:23-27)

7. *Jesus Exercised Power over Evil
Spirits.* (Matthew 5:21-28, 8:28-33,
12:22-23, 17:14-20, Mark 1:21)

8. *Jesus Exercised Power over Heaven &
the Afterlife.* (Mark 9:2-8, Acts 1:6-11)

9. *Jesus Demonstrated the Ability to Read
Minds and Know Other People's
Experiences (which is a fulfillment of
prophesy from Isaiah 11:1-4).* (Matthew
9:2-4, 12:25, Luke 9:47, John 1:47-51,
4:16-18, 6:64, 13:21-27)

10. *Jesus Foretold Future Events.*
(Matthew 16:21, 24:1-2, 24:34-35, 26:2,
26:11-13, 26:21-22, 26:31-32, 26:61,
Mark 13, Luke 19:41-44, 21:24, 21:20-

28, 23:28-30, John 2:18-22, 13:21-27, 13:33, 13:38, 14:26)

Only God can perform genuine miracles because only God, as the Creator of the natural world, has the power to command it. The fact that Jesus showed mastery of every area of the natural and supernatural order in His brief three-year ministry is significant.

7. *Jesus's Victory over Death*

Of all Jesus's miracles, the most important one is, undoubtedly, His resurrection. Jesus claimed to be God, the Creator of the universe and the only way for mankind to be in a relationship with God. Jesus's victory over death backs up His claim to be God in a big way!

There is more evidence for the resurrection of Jesus Christ than for any other single event in the entire Bible.

"AND IF CHRIST HAS NOT BEEN RAISED, OUR PREACHING IS USELESS AND SO IS YOUR FAITH."

I CORINTHIANS 15:14

The resurrection of Christ is hugely important for our ability to have faith in Him.

Below I highlight a few of the events surrounding Jesus's resurrection which provide ample evidence to the truth of this event.

1. ***The earliest manuscripts in our possession today that record the crucifixion and resurrection of Jesus were written and in circulation within the lifetimes of the eye-witnesses.*** In other words, the event itself and the surrounding events were still remembered by those living in Israel at that time. If such wild accounts had been false or easily disproven by someone just saying, "Nope. I remember it all, and it didn't happen that way," the movement would have met a swift end. (Matthew—within 20 years, Mark—within 30 years, Luke—within 30 or 40 years, John—within 20-30 years.)

2. ***Jesus was medically proven to have actually, physically died.*** He wasn't just in a coma or something like that. John 19:32-37 states, *"The soldiers therefore came and broke the legs of the first man who had been crucified with Jesus, and then those of the other. But when they came to Jesus and found that he was already dead, they did not break his*

legs. Instead, one of the soldiers pierced Jesus' side with a spear, bringing a sudden flow of blood and water. The man who saw it has given testimony, and his testimony is true. He knows that he tells the truth, and he testifies so that you also may believe. These things happened so that the Scripture would be fulfilled: 'Not one of his bones will be broken,"'[5] and, as another Scripture says, *"They will look on the one they have pierced."*[6]

This flow of 'blood and water' from Jesus's body was likely blood and fluid from a buildup around Jesus's heart created in cases of asphyxiation. When the soldiers pierced Jesus's side, they pierced this sack and, likely, His lungs and heart, too. He would most certainly be dead. Besides, Roman soldiers were experts in death and, if they did not perform their executioner duties and let one of the prisoners live, they faced death themselves. Another possibility exists, though, to explain the blood and water. Plasma, which is clear like water, will separate from the blood in our bodies after we die—but only after we die. So, the water mentioned might have

---

[5] *Psalm 34:20*
[6] *Zechariah 12:10*

been plasma. If so, this shows, not only that Jesus was indeed dead, but that He'd been dead for quite a while.

3. ***Jesus's body wasn't stolen by His followers.*** The religious and political leaders made sure of that by rolling a huge rock in front of Jesus's tomb, placing Pilate's seal on it, and placing armed guards in front of it. (We're not sure how many guards were there. Estimates suggest between 20 and 100.) Matthew 27:57-66 has the full account. Some key verses are: "*Joseph took the body, wrapped it in a clean linen cloth, and placed it in his own new tomb that he had cut out of the rock. He rolled a big stone in front of the entrance to the tomb.... The next day, the one after Preparation Day, the chief priests and the Pharisees went to Pilate. 'Sir,' they said, 'we remember that while he was still alive that deceiver said, 'After three days I will rise again.' So give the order for the tomb to be made secure until the third day. Otherwise, his disciples may come and steal the body and tell the people that he has been raised from the dead. This last deception will be worse than the first.' 'Take a guard,' Pilate answered. 'Go, make the tomb as secure as you know how.' So they went and*

made the tomb secure by putting a seal on the stone and posting the guard."

4. ***The enemies of Christ attempted a massive cover up.*** Matthew 28:11-15 states, *"...some of the guards went into the city and reported to the chief priests everything that had happened. When the chief priests had met with the elders and devised a plan, they gave the soldiers a large sum of money, telling them, 'You are to say, 'His disciples came during the night and stole him away while we were asleep.' If this report gets to the governor, we will satisfy him and keep you out of trouble.' So the soldiers took the money and did as they were instructed...."* The *trouble* they spoke of was the death of any Roman soldier caught sleeping at his post. The Romans weren't exactly known for their forgiving spirits. So... if the disciples stole the body while the soldiers slept, how did the soldiers know who had done it? And, if they were really asleep, how did 20 or more trained guards sleep through all the noise caused by the rolling away of that massive stone from the tomb's entrance?

5. ***Immediately after Jesus's death, His followers seemed to give up.*** They reacted as anyone would if the one they

had believed to be the Savior of the world had suddenly met a very brutal end at the hands of the enemy. They went into hiding (John 20:19). Now that the leader of their revolt was dead, their lives were in danger from the religious leaders who could kill them for being blasphemers—the same reason used to crucify Jesus. Obviously, the disciples weren't trying to fake anything or start a new religion. But then, suddenly—upon seeing Jesus alive again and realizing His triumph was over not only physical death, but the spiritual death of all mankind—they were so excited and zealous and outspoken that nobody could shut them up (Acts 3-4). *"For we cannot help but speaking about what we have seen and heard"* (Acts 4:20).

5. ***Most of Jesus's disciples and many who followed later were martyred.*** They died still confessing that Jesus was God, the Messiah, the Savior of mankind, and that He had, indeed, conquered death by coming back to life on the third day as He had predicted. Those who lived closest to the evidence of the truth were one hundred percent convinced. Stephen was stoned and some 2,000 other Christians suffered at the time of Stephen's persecution, circa 35 A.D.

Here are a few examples:

- James the Great (Son of Zebedee) was beheaded in 44 A.D.
- Philip the Apostle was crucified in 54 A.D.
- Matthew was killed with a halberd (a long, double-headed axe) in 60 A.D.
- James the Just was beaten to death with a club after being crucified and stoned.
- Matthias was stoned and beheaded.
- Andrew, St. Peter's brother, was crucified.
- Mark was beaten to death.
- Peter was crucified upside-down.
- Apostle Paul was beheaded in Rome.
- Jude was crucified.
- Bartholomew was crucified.
- Thomas the Apostle was killed with a spear.
- Luke the Evangelist was hanged.
- Simon the Zealot was crucified in 74 A.D.

(Note: According to legend, John the Evangelist was cooked in boiling hot oil but survived. He was the only one of the original twelve Apostles who was not, technically, martyred).

8. ***Over 500 eye-witnesses saw Jesus alive after He had died on the cross.*** I Corinthians 15:6 states, *"After that, he appeared to more than five hundred of the brothers at the same time, most of whom are still living, though some have fallen asleep."* Again, if these people were still alive and if this was a lie, wouldn't *somebody* have said something?

9. ***If Jesus hadn't risen from the dead and if the disciples had no chance at all to steal the body, why didn't the religious and political leaders simply produce the body?*** They had control over the tomb. They certainly had sufficient reason to want Jesus's followers squelched, and producing Jesus's body would have quickly disproven that He'd come back to life. So why didn't they? Because *there was no body to be found*. It was gone—up and walking around. Alive.

The evidences for the veracity of the resurrection are many, and these are only a few. But the resurrection of Christ is a pivotal point that can neither be overlooked nor rejected if we are to be secure in our faith. I Corinthians 15:17 states, *"And if Christ has not been raised, your faith is futile; you are still in your sins."* Thankfully, we have more than enough proof that Jesus Christ conquered death and that we, too, are "more than conquerors" through Him. *"No, in all these things we are more than conquerors through him who loved us,"* (Romans 8:37).

8. Jesus Among Other Gods

Though the evidence for Jesus being God is as astounding as it is lengthy, one simply need compare Jesus to the alternatives to see that He stands out from the crowd of would-be saviors. Lots of religious figures have come and gone claiming to have the answer to obtaining a relationship with God and/or spiritual purity:

- Buddha claimed that, through meditation and self-denial, one can eventually attain a higher plane of consciousness, escape the cycle of death and rebirth, and eventually make it to Nirvana.

- Joseph Smith claimed one's salvation depends on how well you follow the laws and practices set out in the Bible and the Book of Mormon.

- Muhammed claimed one's salvation depends on how well one follows the teachings he set forth in the Quran (the Islamic law).

- Hindus assert that one attains 'moksha' (or union with God) through self-realization and by following certain Hindu practices aimed at removing earthly obstacles.

- Paganism, Wicca, and other similar varieties of Spiritualism insist that enlightenment (either becoming your own god and/or becoming unified with the spiritual realm) is attained through meditation, the casting of spells, practicing divination, and/or performing a variety of other interesting rituals and rites….

By now you should be detecting a pattern. Every single other religion has one very basic thing in common: they believe that human beings, despite how flawed and limited in understanding, are somehow capable of earning our own salvation, spiritual enlightenment, or purity by what we do. If we're just good enough, dedicated enough, self-sacrificing enough, we'll get there… at least, that's what they say….

ONLY JESUS PROVIDED A WAY FOR A SINFUL, CREATED BEING TO BE RECONCILED WITH A PERFECT, CREATOR GOD.

But one Man stands out from the rest; one faith system is unique: faith in Jesus Christ. Only Jesus provided an *actual*, *reasonable*, and *verifiable* way for a sinful, created being to be reconciled with a perfect, Creator God—His own death in our place, His victory over the grave, and His offer of a saving love-relationship with us. Every other religion insists we must be good, follow the rules, and earn our right to be saved. But this is impossible.

Can I, on my own, ever work myself up to such a state of perfection that I can be in God's presence without getting zapped? I am linear, after all—stuck in time. And it's certainly not the case that I've never sinned. So, even if I somehow manage to never sin from this moment until the end of my days, I'll still have those early sins on my record. I can't go back and blot them out. I can't make up for them. I can't buy their pardon. I sinned long before I knew of a reason not to—before I knew what sin was. And, even if I could manage to overcome my flaws long enough to clean myself up (which is a pretty backwards, mind-warping concept in and of itself), how would I know when I got there? Furthermore, if I can't make myself 'good enough' (whatever that means), what then?

Consider what happens when something filthy comes in contact with something pure. If I took a glass of pure, clean, filtered water and put just one tiny drop of sewage in it, would the water still be clean and pure—safe to drink? No.

Filth, like sin, contaminates everything it touches, spreading like a cancer. So, the mere idea of something filthy coming into contact with something pure, without having to first be purified, is utter foolishness. It simply doesn't make sense, even from a human perspective.

Because God is Holy, He can't allow non-holiness into His presence—not because our sin makes Him not love us, but because our sin makes us vulnerable.

OUR SIN PUTS US IN EXTREME DANGER.

Unlike pure water, God cannot be 'contaminated' by us. We just don't have that kind of power over Him. But, our sin does put *us* in extreme danger. When an impure being comes into God's full presence, he or she is *destroyed* (Exodus 33:20)! The Bible calls God a *"consuming fire"* (Deuteronomy 4:24 & Hebrews 12:29) and whoever is not protected by Christ's perfect, sinless blood will be *"burned like chaff in an unquenchable fire"* (Luke 3:17).[7] So, our sin puts us on a direct, one-way path to our utter destruction—to an eternity in Hell.

But Jesus—*and only Jesus*—offers a detour.

---

[7] This kind of fire doesn't belong to Satan. Fire belongs to God. It's a part of His nature. And it will destroy whatever enters His presence without the protection of Christ's righteousness.

The Jesus Christ of the Bible stands alone—standing apart from every single other religious figure ever known to man—claiming that, not only is He God incarnate, but His death and resurrection paves the way for mankind to enter into a loving relationship with a perfect God.

"That which was from the beginning, which we have heard, which we have seen with our eyes, which we have looked at and our hands have touched—this we pr oclaim concerning the Word of life. The life appeared; we have seen it and testify to it, and we proclaim to you the eternal life, which was with the Father and has appeared to us. We proclaim to you what we have seen and heard, so that you also may have fellowship with us. And our fellowship is with the Father and with his Son, Jesus Christ" (I John 1:1-3).

TALK IT OUT

1. In what ways did Jesus claim to be God? Did He back up this claim? If so, how?

2. What do Jesus's miracles tell us about Him?
3. Why is our faith in Jesus's victory over death of vital importance to our faith in Him—indeed, to our very salvation?

4. How does Jesus contrast with other religious figures of today?

VIII
HOW CAN I BE SURE JESUS SAVED ME?

We are imperfect and have no way to earn our own salvation. In our natural state, the only thing we can do in response to our sins is to die for them. But God was not satisfied with that. He loves us too much to leave us in our sin, doomed to destruction. So God became a man—Jesus Christ—and lived a perfect life on Earth. In doing so, He made Himself able to pay the price for the sin of all mankind. When He died in our place and rose again, He conquered the requirement of death for us (John 3:16). He extends the offer of rescue to any who will receive it. All we have to do is believe and accept.

"If you declare with your mouth, 'Jesus is Lord,' and believe in your heart that God raised him from the dead, you will be saved" (Romans 10:9).

The only way for us to have a relationship with God is through Jesus Christ (John 14:6). That is because Jesus (who is God) was the only one who was able to make a way for a sinful being like you and me to get into God's presence without being burned to a crisp.

However, because Jesus is a real *Being*, and not just a benign *belief*, what we should be looking for—indeed, expecting—is an actual relationship with a Person, not just a tacit commitment to a set of religious ideals and statements. Neither should we expect our emotions to somehow confirm our salvation. Nowhere does Scripture tell us that our emotions are a legitimate measuring rod of truth, so don't assume your request for salvation "didn't take" just because you didn't feel any differently after you asked.

The answer to the question, "How can I know Jesus saved me?" is two-fold:

1. ***Accepting the Truth.***
   Certain facts apply: Jesus is God, He died in your place and conquered death by rising from the grave, and He promises to save anyone who believes in Him and desires a relationship with Him. *"Here I am! I stand at the door and knock. If anyone hears my voice and opens the door, I will come in and eat with that person, and they with me"* (Revelation 5:20). The first part of answering this question is by believing the facts about Jesus.

2. ***Choosing Him.***
   Once you know Jesus can save you and wants to save you, you must decide for

yourself whether you are going to follow Him—to accept His payment for your sins, to accept His offer of a new life as one of His children, and to surrender your will to His.

This is the relationship—the development of interpersonal knowledge—that I have been talking about since the beginning of this book. It's more than mere belief. It is an ongoing surrender to a Person. But as scary as that might sound, it is also incredibly exhilarating! This is the deepest, most challenging, most fulfilling, most crazy-cool relationship you will ever have!

Some of this book's readers will know for certain they already have a growing, dynamic relationship with Jesus Christ and are confident of what will happen to them at the point of death. Others might not be so sure. If you're one of the latter, you need to know that the decision is up to you—and only you. You can't coast into Heaven on your parents' or pastor's relationship with God. You have to have your own. And the only way to have a relationship with God is to accept Jesus as the Lord of your life. Jesus said, *"I am the way and the truth and the life. No one comes to the Father except through me,"* (John 14:6).

Only by a relationship with Jesus can you get to God—not by adhering to some religion, by doing good things, or by avoiding bad things. So give your heart to God and welcome Jesus into your life. I will show you how to start that relationship. But, I'm going to deviate from the norm for a book like this and *not* give you a pre-written sinner's prayer. I don't want to encourage the idea that just saying a certain set of words works like some kind of magic spell that gets you into Heaven. It doesn't work like that. (Although, if you at any time accepted Jesus via a pre-written sinner's prayer, that's perfectly fine—as long as you meant what you said.)

There is no "right" or "wrong" way to ask Jesus into your heart and life. It's not a formula. You are starting a relationship with a Person. Of course, this relationship is unique in that it is between you and your Creator and would-be Savior. So, there are a few key things you need to recognize, accept, and confess before Jesus when you pray. I will outline them here, but the prayer itself is up to you. You can do it. Just speak from the heart. He'll hear you.

- ***Admit you need a Savior.***
  Romans 3:23 says, *"For all have sinned and fallen short of the glory of God."* That means you. And as long as you stay in your sins, trying in vain to save yourself or ignore the problem, you will never find peace with God. Isaiah 64:6 says, *"All of us have become like one who is unclean, and all our*

righteous acts are like filthy rags; we all shrivel up like a leaf, and like the wind our sins sweep us away." So, time to fess up. Get real and get it all out. He already knows, anyway. Now it's time for you to recognize your faults and lay yourself bare before God.

- **_Recognize what Jesus did for you._**
  "For God so loved the world that he gave his one and only Son, that whoever believes in him shall not perish but have eternal life" (John 3:16). Philippians 2:8 reads, *"And being found in appearance as a man, he humbled himself and became obedient to death—even death on a cross!"* The only reason you have any right to approach God today is because of what Jesus did for you. The cost to Him was excruciating and agonizing on every level—physically, emotionally, and spiritually. Though He was innocent, He willingly went to the cross in your place. *"But they kept shouting, 'Crucify him! Crucify him!' For the third time [Pilate] spoke to them: 'Why? What crime has this man committed? I have found in him no grounds for the death penalty. Therefore I will have him punished and then release him.' But with loud shouts they insistently demanded that he be crucified, and their shouts prevailed"* (Luke 23: 21-23).

- ***Invite Jesus to sit on the throne of your life.***

  "Yet to all who received him, to those who believed in his name, he gave the right to become children of God" (John 1:12). This is where you ask Jesus to forgive you from your sins and rescue you from their hold on your life. And though Jesus makes this offer freely, accepting it will cost you everything. It is not something to be entered into lightly, thinking, "Well, I'll give this a try for a week or so and, if all my problems don't disappear, I'll try something else." No. This is the beginning of a relationship with a real Being, not a trial run for a belief system or an operational strategy. You must approach with humility, asking on bended knee that He change your heart and mind from the inside out. Of course, He will accept you as you are. You don't have to clean yourself up first; He wants to help you with that. But don't forget who you're talking to—the God of the Universe, your Creator, and the One who suffered agonizing pain in your place. From here on out, if God is to be on the throne of your life, you will need to follow His lead and be obedient to what He tells you.

- ***Thank Jesus for forgiving you and welcoming you into your new life in Him!***

  I John 1:9 tells us, *"If we confess our sins, he is faithful and just and will forgive us our sins and purify us from all unrighteousness."* This is a promise! If you just gave your heart to God, He promises to set us free from the chains of our sins. You can now approach God with confidence under the protection of Christ's righteousness. And He makes an additional promise: *"God has said, 'Never will I leave you; never will I forsake you'"* (Hebrews 13:5). He is yours and you are His forever!

If you have prayed these things, whether today or years ago, you may be wondering: How do I know if it 'took'? Did I do it right?

Do you think that the God who chose to become a man (leaving Heaven behind), lived a human life as an outcast, suffered incredible torture, and watched His friends betray Him to die in disgrace in agony—all to give you the right to know Him and love Him—would now say, "Oh, sorry. You didn't read the sinner's prayer right, so you can't come in." Or, "Oh, I see there is a bit of doubt in your heart, so the deal's off." Not at all. He bent over backwards to save you. He says that even the teeniest bit of a relationship (of faith) is enough to, not only save you and welcome you into Heaven when you die, but to guide you and protect you and comfort you for the rest of your life (Luke 17:6). And once you have a relationship with God, nobody can take it away.

"And this is the testimony: God has given us eternal life, and this life is in his Son. Whoever has the Son has life; whoever does not have the Son of God does not have life. I write these things to you who believe in the name of the Son of God so that you may know that you have eternal life" (I John 5:11-13).

When I was about five years old, I prayed along with a lady at a VBS at a mission in Bolivia (my

IF YOU HAVE JESUS, YOU HAVE ETERNAL LIFE.

parents were missionaries in Argentina at the time), and I accepted Jesus into my heart that day. But, for the next several years, I prayed a similar prayer every day, afraid Jesus would leave me if I wasn't exactly perfect. I know now that Jesus gladly saved me on that very first day, and He never once left. He promises the same thing to you, and as you get to know Him better and learn to trust Him through the ups and downs of life, you'll grow deeper and deeper in the assurance that His love for you far surpasses your love for Him. And once He's got your heart, He refuses to let go!

Romans 8:37-39 says, *"No, in all these things we are more than conquerors through him who loved us. For I am convinced that neither death nor life, neither angels nor demons, neither the present nor the future, nor any powers, neither height nor depth, nor anything else in all creation, will be able to separate us from the love of God that is in Christ Jesus our Lord."*

Ephesians 3:17b-19 says, *"And I pray that you, being rooted and established in love, may have power, together with all the saints, to grasp how wide and long and high and deep is the love of Christ, and to know this love that surpasses knowledge—that you may be filled to the measure of all the fullness of God."*

TALK IT OUT

1. How does a relationship with a person differ from agreement with a set of beliefs about a person?

2. When it comes to your own relationship with Jesus Christ, where would you say you are?

3. Have you ever been afraid of losing your salvation? Why or why not?

4. Describe how you feel about the idea of moving into your future with Jesus on the throne of your life.

IX
HOW DO I KNOW I HAVE A RELATIONSHIP WITH GOD (AND NOT JUST A SET OF BELIEFS?)

A relationship with a person is far different from having a set of beliefs or following a religion. A relationship changes over time and is unique to the people involved. When you have a relationship with God, the circumstances of life will challenge that relationship—forcing you to either abandon Him or go deeper.

Laurie tells us, "I married in my 20's and shortly thereafter, the marriage fell apart. The divorce was the main thing in my life as a young Christian that really tested everything that I knew and believed about God. I clung to the Lord in order to get through the divorce and face single motherhood. My faith was tested to the utmost and God took me to the end of myself so that I had nowhere to turn but to Him."

Edd shares, "In my senior year in high school, my very best friend was killed in a car wreck. I was supposed to be with him, but got grounded the day before. I actually felt guilty that I wasn't with him the night he died. From then on, I felt that I should experience each new opportunity that life placed before me—whether right or wrong. I never did anything I thought would hurt someone else, but I had little concern for myself. ...Though I knew of God from the time I was a young child, I actually met God in a cane field in Vietnam. My helicopter was shot down and my Crew Chief was blown out of the helicopter. His body was found 3 days later after we were shot down. My Observer was still alive when we hit the ground. He died about 20 minutes after we crashed. I laid beside my helicopter for over an hour with only one round of ammunition in my pistol. I could hear the enemy moving all around me in that cane field. I wondered if my parents would ever even know which country I was killed in, since we flew over the border areas of three different nations. It was then, in that cane field, that the God I knew of, became the God I actually met spiritually for the very first time. It was that day that He became real to me!!!"

What is Faith in God?

Faith is not an abstract concept. And the kind of faith that saves is not mere *belief* in God or Jesus, of the variety: "I believe God exists and Jesus once lived." Saving faith goes much, much deeper.

"You believe that there is one God. Good! Even the demons believe that—and shudder" (James 2:19).

If you were to make a list of the most important things in life, what would be at the top of that list? No matter what you believe about God, you'd likely put things like friends and family very near the top, higher up than things like "chocolate" or "my car." That's because it's *relationship* that makes human beings feel the most happy and secure. So, when I read the word "faith" in the Bible, I often replace that word with "relationship," and it makes more sense to me.

For example: Ephesians 3:11 states, *"In him and through faith in him we may approach God with freedom and confidence."* Now, read it like this: "In him and through [my relationship with] him [I] may approach God with freedom and confidence." See the difference? The kind of faith God desires is a type of positive, loving, trusting relationship—one that grows over time and develops a deeper knowledge of the Person of Jesus Christ.

We can know Jesus in a way similar to how we know people. For example, I know my mom really, really well. Of course, that's not to say that I know *everything* about her or that I don't have anything else to learn. But let's say someone called me up and said, "I just saw your mom! She has run off with a Russian model and is on her way to Bulgaria!" Now, because I know my mom, my first reaction would be to say. "No. That's not my mom. I *know* you're wrong." Why would I have this kind of confidence? What facts do I really have in this moment? I don't know where, precisely, my mom is. I don't know whom she is with. I don't know what she is doing. However, because I know *her*, I *know* she's not running off to Bulgaria with a Russian model! I am so certain of this, in fact, I would pass off the caller as some freak, and I wouldn't bother calling her up to check the story.

This is the kind of "faith" God wants us to develop in Him through His Son Jesus Christ. It's not dependent on particular, *minute* facts that we have at our immediate disposal (although certain facts matter a great deal—like those that pertain to His identity as God, for example). We may not know why Jesus is asking us to speak to that stranger on the bus or turn down the invitation to that party, but because we know *Him*, we know He has a very good reason, and we trust Him enough to obey.

The Bible tells us: *"Now faith is the substance of things hoped for, the evidence of things not seen"* (Hebrews 11:1). Faith is both something with real "substance" and it is also evidence, in and of itself. Relationship itself, I believe, is the "substance" referred to in that verse, and reconciliation with God is what we "hope for."

The Bible tells us that curiosity about God is not possible unless God is actively at work, drawing us toward Him. *"No one comes to me unless the Father who sent me draws him"* (John 6:44). It also says that my faith doesn't even originate with me but with God (Romans 12:3 & Hebrews 12:2). So, faith in Jesus can't be something we are given by our parents or that we get from society or that we make up because we're lonely. This kind of faith is a relationship with an actual *Being*, not a commitment to a mere *belief*. Furthermore, feeling convicted of sin also comes from God (John 16:8 & Hebrews 4:12).

So, how do we know our relationships are real? Because we've had actual experiences with a real Being—another living, conscious personality. Think back over your life and ask yourself: Have I ever heard God speaking to me or teaching me something? Has God ever taken an active role in my life? Have I been drawn to faith in God? Made aware of spiritual truths? Been curious about God and spiritual things? Have I ever felt convicted of sin?

If you answer yes to any of these questions, your answer is evidence that the Holy Spirit has been active in your life. So, in this way, your faith is also evidence, just like Hebrews 11:1 says. So, faith is a relationship with a Person with whom

IF YOU ANSWER YES TO ANY OF THESE QUESTIONS, YOUR ANSWER IS EVIDENCE THAT THE HOLY SPIRIT HAS BEEN ACTIVE IN YOUR LIFE.

you've had multiple experiences over your life. Some of these experiences happened before you even knew He existed and before you put your trust in Him. Others are happening in this very moment. God is deeply involved in your life, and He is always at work in your heart and mind, continually drawing you closer and giving you wisdom. (Ever feel like you could use more wisdom? Just read James 1:5.)

If you have asked Jesus into your life and accepted His payment on the cross in exchange for your sins but are still doubting your salvation, you're focusing on yourself too much and not enough on Jesus. You don't have to *do* anything for your salvation—except accept it. He did everything else. Ephesians 2:8-9 says, *"For it is by grace you have been saved, through faith—and this not from yourselves, it is the gift of God—not by works, so that no one can boast."*

At the same time, your response to God's calling you into relationship with Him is of utmost importance. A relationship is a two-way street. So, if He is calling, you had better answer.

A RELATIONSHIP IS A TWO-WAY STREET. SO, IF HE IS CALLING, YOU HAD BETTER ANSWER.

In Mark 10:15, Jesus says, *"I tell you the truth, anyone who will not receive the kingdom of God like a little child will never enter it."* Your belief and acceptance is of utmost importance. When the Bible talks about believing in Jesus, it means believing Jesus is indeed God and your Creator, giving Him your love and trust, and being willing to get to know Him through a life-long, committed relationship.

So, take a good look at who you are and compare that to who He is. Then decide if you need Him and want to give Him the reins of your life. That's it. James 4:10 says, *"Humble yourselves before God and He will lift you up."*

TALK IT OUT

1. Up until now, have you had a relationship with Jesus or just a set of beliefs about Him?

2. How can you know your relationship with Jesus is real?

3. What struggles have you encountered within your relationship with Jesus? Have they been resolved? If so, how?

4. What assurances do you have regarding your relationship with Jesus Christ?

5. Is your faith growing? If so, how do you know? If not, what can you to ensure that it does?

X
THE SURRENDERED LIFE

You may have heard people speaking about "committing" themselves to Jesus or "recommitting" their lives to God. As great as that sounds, it's only a half-step in the right direction. Consider the following question:

What is the difference between *commitment* and *surrender*?

Which is fuller? Which demands more of you? Which one leaves no wiggle-room? No holding back?

You can, for example, commit your drinking problem to God, all the while withholding from Him access to your sexual lust. Or, you might commit yourself to Him in areas of purity, while holding onto your habit of gossiping about people behind their backs. Maybe you are comfortable giving Jesus your money— faithfully tithing every month, but you stubbornly guard your time—refusing to spend time in the Word or helping out a friend in need.

Commitment says, "God, You can have this area of my life… but not that one." Surrender lays everything bare before Him. Surrender says, "Whatever You'll have of me... it's Yours. Take it all."

> THEREFORE, IF ANYONE
> IS IN CHRIST, THE NEW
> CREATION HAS COME:
> THE OLD HAS GONE,
> THE NEW IS HERE!
> II CORINTHIANS 5:17

God does not look lightly on half efforts and riding the fence when it comes to how we respond to Him. With God, it has to be all or nothing.

"I know your deeds, that you are neither cold nor hot. I wish you were either one or the other! So, because you are lukewarm—neither hot nor cold—I am about to spit you out of my mouth" (Revelations 3:15-16).

The apostle, Paul, knew this kind of selflessness and faith in God was difficult. He wrote the following:

"So I find this law at work: Although I want to do good, evil is right there with me. For in my inner being I delight in God's law; but I see another law at work in me, waging war against the law of my mind and making me a prisoner of the law of sin at work within me. What a

wretched man I am! Who will rescue me from this body that is subject to death? Thanks be to God, who delivers me through Jesus Christ our Lord" (Romans 7:21-25a)!

Paul experienced trials far more horrifying than anything you or I are likely to face but, as he learned to trust the Lord through each of them, his fear morphed into assurance and joy. He said, *"For this reason I also suffer these things, but I am not ashamed; for I know whom I have believed and I am convinced that He is able to guard what I have entrusted to Him until that day"* (II Timothy 1:12).

Paul knew that anything he entrusted to Jesus would be guarded faithfully—his possessions, his freedom, his loved ones, his sacrifices—even his life and death.

Setting Your Desires to the Side

Society teaches us to pursue whatever we desire. Individuality and ambition are praised. The maxim, "Follow your heart," is in everything from Disney movies to self-help programs to natural food ads. But the prophet Jeremiah said, *"The heart is deceitful above all things and beyond cure. Who can understand it"* (Jeremiah 17:9)?

"Each person is tempted when they are dragged away by their own evil desire and enticed. Then, after desire has conceived, it gives birth to sin; and sin, when it is full-grown, gives birth to death"* (James 1:14-15).

CONTROL YOUR DESIRES; DO NOT LET THEM CONTROL YOU.

John the Baptist was Jesus's cousin and the messenger who heralded the coming of the long-awaited Messiah. He had a flourishing ministry and many disciples. But John realized that, if he was to continue to do God's will, he would have to take a back seat to Jesus. He said, *"A person can receive only what is given them from heaven. ...[Jesus] must become greater; I must become less"* John 3:27-30.

"Therefore, I urge you, brothers and sisters, in view of God's mercy, to offer your bodies as a living sacrifice, holy and pleasing to God—this is your true and proper worship. Do not conform to the pattern of this world, but be transformed by the renewing of your mind. Then you will be able to test and approve what God's will is—his good, pleasing and perfect will" (Romans 12:1-2).

Saying No to Sin

Today's culture continually tries to redefine morality to fit their own values and desires. But Jesus holds us to a much higher standard—Himself. Sin is when we miss the mark of what God has asked us to do. Sin is when we choose what we want over what God has commanded. Sin is also a measuring rod for whether or not you love Christ. Jesus said, *"Anyone who loves me will obey my teaching"* (John 14:23a). God's command to be obedient is absolute, because He knows what happens when we allow sin to rule us.

"For the wages of sin is death, but the gift of God is eternal life in Christ Jesus our Lord" (Romans 6:23).

If it wasn't for our sin, Jesus would not have had to die. He died to pay the penalty—death—for my sin and your sin. Keep that in mind whenever you feel tempted to do what you know you ought not do.

"For all have sinned and fall short of the glory of God, and all are justified freely by his grace through the redemption that came by Christ Jesus" (Romans 3:23-24).

And don't forget that you were made for more than the things of this world. You are far too valuable (worth Christ's own life) to waste yourself on the things that seek to destroy you. If you have accepted Jesus Christ as your Savior and Friend, then He has made you a "new creation."

"Therefore, if anyone is in Christ, the new creation has come: The old has gone, the new is here" (II Corinthians 5:17)!

YOU ARE WORTH CHRIST'S OWN LIFE, AND YOU WERE DESIGNED TO DO GOOD WORKS AND TO BE A BLESSING TO OTHERS.

"As for you, you were dead in your transgressions and sins, in which you used to live when you followed the ways of this world and of the ruler of the kingdom of the air, the spirit who is now at work in those who are disobedient. All of us also lived among them at one time, gratifying the cravings of our flesh and following its desires and thoughts. Like the rest, we were by nature deserving of wrath. But because of his great love for us, God, who is rich in mercy, made us alive with Christ even when we were dead in transgressions.... For it is by grace you have been saved, through faith—and this is not from yourselves, it is the gift of God—not by works, so that no one can boast. For we are God's handiwork, created in Christ Jesus to do

good works, which God prepared in advance for us to do" (Ephesians 2:1-10).

Repentance

Time to get real. There will be times when you will make mistakes. You will fall to temptation. You will make errors in judgment that will cause hurt to others. That does not mean you have lost your salvation. Even long periods of time wandering away from Christ is not enough for Him to give up on you. But you can cause great harm to yourself, to others, and to your relationship with God by choosing your own way over His. This is why God repeatedly calls us to repentance.

"Peter replied, 'Repent and be baptized, every one of you, in the name of Jesus Christ for the forgiveness of your sins. And you will receive the gift of the Holy Spirit'" (Acts 2:38).

If you've blown it, now is the time to confess that to the Lord and make it right. Jesus promises that, if we confess our sin to Him, He will forgive us.

"If we confess our sins, he is faithful and just and will forgive us our sins and purify us from all unrighteousness" (I John 1:9).

Jesus's desire is to rescue us, not condemn us.

"For God did not send his Son into the world to condemn the world, but to save the world through him" (John 3:17).

But He does insist that we stop whatever we're doing that is separating us from Him.

"Then neither do I condemn you," Jesus declared. *"Go now and leave your life of sin"* (John 8:11).

So stop whatever it is you're not supposed to be doing and start doing what you know you should be doing. If you're not sure what that is, delve into the Word, get real in your prayer life, and ask Him to show you. Then obey. It may feel complicated, but it's actually very simple. It comes down to a choice.

"But if a wicked person turns away from all the sins they have committed and keeps all my decrees and does what is just and right, that person will surely live; they will not die" (Ezekiel 18:21).

TALK IT OUT

1. Do you struggle with surrendering to Christ? Why or why not?

2. Are you willing to trust your heart, your mind, and your future to Jesus Christ? Will you give Him your attitudes and opinions, temptations and lusts, desires and dreams?

3. What practical steps can you take to help you say no to sin?

4. Is there an area in your life that requires repentance? What do you think God's response will be to your request for forgiveness?

XI
FREEDOM IN JESUS CHRIST

" *I* t is for freedom that Christ has set us free. Stand firm, then, and do not let yourselves be burdened again by a yoke of slavery" (Galatians 5:1).

Here's a paradoxical truth: We are at our *most free* when we *surrender* to Jesus Christ.

Sound strange? Consider the following: The kind of freedom we are looking for is not about being *free from* something, but rather, being *free to do/be* something. For example, if you are free from gravity, you will not feel very free. You will feel trapped by the fact that you are floating up into the atmosphere where, soon, you will no longer be able to breathe. That is not the kind of "freedom" any of us wants. Gravity, because it restrains us in one way, frees us in another. It *frees us to* go about life in a normal, healthy way, firmly planted on the ground.

Here is another idea to consider: Freedom is not about being or doing anything you want; it is about becoming the kind of being you were designed to be. For example: A fish might be morally free to hang out in a tree for a while, but a fish would not desire that kind of freedom, for one simple fact: he is a fish. A fish is *freest* in the water—going about life in a fish-like way, according to the way he was designed.

Someone once asked me, "Is sex before marriage morally wrong?" I answered, "Not if you're a dog." Dogs can have sex with any other dog they want (and even with table legs) without ever considering marriage and never experience a moment's guilt about it. But people are different kinds of beings. Unlike dogs, we have complicated relationships, child-raising needs, and family structures that dogs don't have to consider. God has given us particular rules about sex that He didn't give to dogs. Therefore, sex before marriage *for a person* creates all kinds of moral complications—because of the types of beings that we are. God designed marriage to provide an earthly, triune model (i.e. man, woman, and Christ) of a Heavenly, triune God (i.e. Father, Son, and Holy Spirit). So, to misunderstand or abuse sex or marriage is evidence that we do not understand who God is or who we are as His children.

WE ARE *MOST FREE*
WHEN WE *SURRENDER*
TO JESUS CHRIST.

People were designed by a loving God to exist in relationship with Him. Therefore, it is only through relationship with your Creator that you will find true freedom.

Whatever we feel we might have lost in our surrender to Christ is nothing compared to the riches He offers. It's about the equivalent of handing over a broken Matchbox minivan for a genuine, brand-new Lamborghini. You're not even going to remember the tiny minivan. No matter how attached you now feel to the things and desires and opinions that are out of line with what He says are good and right and true, once you hand those things over to Christ and He teaches you to see with His eyes, you're going to feel pretty foolish for holding on so tightly to them for so long.

"You will make known to me the path of life; in Your presence is fullness of joy; in Your right hand there are pleasures forever" (Psalm 16:11).

Jesus offers you complete freedom in Him! That is incredibly good news! But there are forces in this world that will seek to rob you of your freedom.

"This matter arose because some false believers had infiltrated our ranks to spy on the freedom we have in Christ Jesus and to make us slaves" (Galatians 2:4).

Therefore, you must be diligent and on the watch for false teachings. The Bible tells us to be *"shrewd as snakes and as innocent as doves"*

(Matthew 10:16). One way to do this is to stay engrained in Scripture.

Laurie said, "I experimented with a few different denominations and non-denominational churches and learned about various Christian theologies that are out there. But deep inside I felt that same dedication and love for the Truth that my mom instilled in me. So I kept going back to Scripture and testing all the new things I was learning. One by one, I eliminated philosophies and beliefs that did not match up to Scripture."

"Now the Berean Jews were of more noble character than those in Thessalonica, for they received the message with great eagerness and examined the Scriptures every day to see if what Paul said was true" (Acts 17:11).

Another way to avail yourself of God's wisdom is through prayer and reliance on the Holy Spirit.

Liwen says, "I went to a very liberal college, but I did find good Christian fellowships and a church and made many good friends. I also had a mentor who was a staff member with Campus Crusade who devoted her time in helping me grow in my faith. Even though I had been going to a Bible teaching church prior to college, she was the one who taught me about the role of the Holy Spirit."

"But the Advocate, the Holy Spirit, whom the Father will send in my name, will teach you all things and will remind you of everything I have said to you" (John 14:26).

I have three kids. One is in college, the other is in high school, and the youngest is in middle school. All three of them have struggled with temptations and worries and confusions of various kinds, but my advice is always the same. I remind them that they have each given their lives to Jesus Christ, and He promises to help them with each struggle as it comes.

"The weapons we fight with are not the weapons of the world. On the contrary, they have divine power to demolish strongholds. We demolish arguments and every pretension that sets itself up against the knowledge of God, and ***we take captive every thought to make it obedient to Christ"*** (II Corinthians 10:4-5) (emphasis added).

The Bible tells us to "take every thought captive." That means every desire, every fear, every worry, every temptation. If Jesus did not give us the ability to do that, He would not have told us to do it. How do we take these stray, destructive thoughts captive? By making them "obedient to Christ." We give them to Him—as often as we have to—every five minutes, if necessary—until He gives us mastery over them.

Do not let your emotions or desires or thoughts control you. Instead, control them. Jesus's presence in your heart gives you power over them:

"For the grace of God has appeared that offers salvation to all people. It teaches us to say 'No' to ungodliness and worldly passions, and to live self-controlled, upright and godly lives in this present age, while we wait for the blessed hope—the appearing of the glory of our great God and Savior, Jesus Christ" (Titus 2:11-13).

Need some pointers to get you going in the right direction? Here is some more friendly advice from our friends, Laurie, Liwen, Edd, and Caryl:

Laurie says, "Don't let your rebellion against your parents or any relational issues influence your quest for the Truth. If you are trying to be independent and want to develop your own faith, be faithful in seeking the Lord through His Word. ...You belong to Christ now. He has a purpose for you, and you won't be truly fulfilled unless you follow Him completely. ...Always have good, strong, mature Christians around you that can answer your questions. Never grab onto something without digging into God's Word as the plumb line to measure all of these things against. Search for sound Biblical teachers and cling to the Lord Jesus as you learn and grow."

Liwen says, "The best advice I can give is to get plugged into a good church and fellowship and surround yourself with mature, growing Christians. And to be sure of what you believe and to keep studying God's word and asking questions and searching for answers."

Edd says, "I would sincerely like to say my near death experience changed my life dramatically that day in that cane field in Southeast Asia... but it didn't. It took many years for my surrender to our Heavenly Father to take place. When I finally fell to my knees, I was in my 50's. Since then, I ask the Lord countless times every day to lead me and allow me to reflect His Glory always and forever!!! My guiding Scripture is Acts 20:24." *"However, I consider my life worth nothing to me; my only aim is to finish the race and complete the task the Lord Jesus has given me—the task of testifying to the good news of God's grace."*

Caryl provides the following four ways to stick close to the Lord:

- **Pray daily!** I don't mean a long, head bowed, eyes closed prayer. You can talk

114 | S. E. Thomas, M.A.

to Him all day long. Even a little 'Help me, Father' before a hard task is prayer. So is 'Thank You, Lord' when something good happens. I Thessalonians 5:17 tells us to pray without ceasing. Little conversations with God all day long keep Him on your mind.

- **Read the Bible daily.** His Word will light your way. Memorize the verses that stand out or especially speak to you that day. Write it down to read several times aloud. Hiding His Word in your heart will help you not to sin against Him! (Psalm 119:11) Being in the Word teaches me how to trust Him more. For instance, are you having a problem with fear? Look up 'fear' and 'afraid' and discover that God tells us 365 times not to be afraid! Once for every day! Isn't that encouraging?

- **Do your best to follow what you know is RIGHT before Him**... paying no attention to what society says is acceptable. Every day we must make choices. Here they are: life or death? Blessings or curses? Right or wrong? Love or hate? There are no grays. It's black or it's white. The Word tells us, "choose life!" (Deuteronomy 30:19) If you flub up, repent, go, and sin no more.

Don't let one little uh-oh make it easier to engage in some bigger wrongdoing the next day.

- **Find a group of like believers with whom you can study the Word and fellowship.** Be loyal and steadfast to these brothers and sisters-in-Christ. If you will do these things, your life will be so much better, filled with peace and joy. You will still have trouble—so long as you are in this world, but you can be of good cheer, for He has overcome the world! (John 16:33)

No matter what your history has been, Jesus is, in this moment, drawing you deeper toward Him. You should respond. Have a good long talk with Him and put Him above every other love in your life. Completely surrender. Next, like Laurie, Liwen, Edd, and Caryl say, make some good choices that will help you strengthen your relationship with Him. Here are some further suggestions:

- Thank Him again for saving your life.

- Find a group of fellow believers to join, and then get involved, such as a youth group or Christian college group. Learn to do life together with other Christians. Remember, we're designed for relationship, and a big part of your spiritual growth will come through deepening your relationships with other believers, learning to love them, learning from them, forgiving them, encouraging them, and exhorting them.

- Worship Him as the Holy One, the Awesome Creator, and the Savior of the World. Worship as often as you can—sing along with the radio, sing in the shower, take a stroll by yourself for a chance to tell Him how wonderful He is.

- Pick a book of the Bible to read and stick to it. Or, look for something in the Bible you'd like to learn more about (maybe you want to study Jesus's miracles or you have a question about God or Heaven you want answered) and then commit to studying until your curiosity is satisfied.

- Examine your prayer life. If it's too rote or bland (or, perhaps, nonexistent) make a change.

- Find a way to serve others. Volunteer at a charity, food bank, or local crisis pregnancy center. *"Religion that God our Father accepts as pure and faultless is this: to look after orphans and widows in their distress and to keep oneself from being polluted by the world"* (James 1:27).

- Look for ways to share Jesus with others. Learn to love other people as He does, and then look for opportunities to serve them and share Jesus with them.

- Talk to God honestly about what's in your heart and mind. What are your doubts? What are your fears? What challenges lay ahead? Where could you use His wisdom?

- Be honest with God about the areas where you're blowing it. I promise, it won't come as a surprise to Him, but He will want to help you set things right.

- Listen to the Holy Spirit's voice in your life. Make the choice to do the right thing, even when it's difficult, even when your friends will ridicule you, even if your girlfriend/boyfriend will leave you, even when it might mean you won't get that job, internship, or spot on the team. As you walk through in obedience through these tough situations, the Holy Spirit's voice in your life will grow louder and making good choices will get easier. (And here's a free tip: God's voice guides, encourages, compels, and draws. Satan's voice drives, goads, bullies, and threatens.)

Keep your eyes, ears, and heart open for new ways to grow deeper in Christ. Remember, it's not a formula. It's not a set of rules you have to follow. You're free to be who God made you to be before God and others! So, it's up to you and Jesus to walk together into this new life He offers!

Remember, life will throw you some curves. Questions will arise that will seem unanswerable. But do not let your fears (fears based on limited information) derail your entire life or your faith in God. They should not have that much power over you. They should be treated as mere encouragements to continue learning and growing in your faith and knowledge of God—opportunities to learn new, exciting truths!

After all, a relationship with a Being can never be replaced or exchanged for another because a relationship an experience, not a belief. Experiences become a part of our history and of ourselves. No one can take your relationship with God away from you any more than they can take away your relationship with your mother or your best friend. So take a deep breath, thank God for loving you enough to draw you deeper into Himself through this experience of searching, and follow the example of the Bereans—eagerly study the Scriptures to be certain that what you've read here today is true.

TALK IT OUT

1. What kind of freedom are you looking for?

2. What kind of freedom does Jesus Christ offer?

3. What practical steps are you going to take to protect and maintain your freedom in Jesus Christ?

BLESSED ARE THOSE
WHO HUNGER AND
THIRST AFTER
RIGHTEOUSNESS, FOR
THEY WILL BE FILLED.

MATTHEW 5:6

RESOURCES

The Apostle's Creed

I believe in God, the Father almighty, creator of heaven and earth. I believe in Jesus Christ, God's only Son, our Lord, who was conceived by the Holy Spirit, born of the Virgin Mary, suffered under Pontius Pilate, was crucified, died, and was buried; he descended into hell. On the third day he rose again; he ascended into heaven, he is seated at the right hand of the Father, and he will come to judge the living and the dead. I believe in the Holy Spirit, the holy catholic and apostolic Church, the communion of saints, the forgiveness of sins, the resurrection of the body, and the life everlasting. Amen.

Recommended Further Reading:

The Bible

You can find many free Bible reading plans through a simple online search or through the sites listed below. Read the Bible in 60 days, 90 days, a year, or two years. It's up to you. The important thing is that you're reading it.

"I Don't Have Enough Faith to Be an Atheist," by Normal L. Geisler and Frank Turek

A book on basic Christian apologetics which deals with scientific and spiritual questions from the existence of the universe to the identity of Jesus Christ.

"The Jesus I Never Knew," by Philip Yancey
Philip Yancey offers a new and different perspective on the life of Christ and His work—His teachings, His miracles, His death and resurrection—and ultimately, who He was and why He came.

"The Pursuit of God" by A. W. Tozer
A masterly study of the inner life by a heart thirsting after God, eager to grasp at least the outskirts of His ways, the abyss of His love for sinners, and the height of His unapproachable majesty.

"Don't Take Love Lying Down," by Brad Henning
If you've ever had a relationship fall apart; if you've been burned and don't understand why; if you wonder what real love is; or maybe this relationship stuff just doesn't make sense to you any more, then this book is for you.

"Blue Like Jazz: Non-religious Thoughts on Christian Spirituality," by Donald Miller
For anyone wondering if the Christian faith is still relevant in a postmodern culture, thirsting for a genuine encounter with a God who is real, or yearning for a renewed sense of passion in life, *Blue Like Jazz* is a fresh and original perspective on life, love, and redemption.

Helpful Websites:

Bible Gateway: www.BibleGateway.com
Read and study the Bible online for free!
Compare multiple versions in multiple
languages and access Bible commentaries,
dictionaries, encyclopedias, maps, and more.

The Fallacy Files: www.FallacyFiles.org
A collection of logical fallacies with
explanations and examples to help you identify
them in your arguments and in the arguments of
others.

Got Questions?: www.GotQuestions.org
A website dedicated to answering your
questions about God, Jesus, and the Bible.

Knowing Jesus: www. Knowing-Jesus.com
A resource that provides devotionals, topical
Bible verse lists, insightful articles, and much
more to help you know Jesus better.

Life's Midterm: www.LifesMidterm.com
A resource for anyone who has questions about
God, life, or how to have a healthy relationship.

Bible Reading Schedules:
www.BackToTheBible.org/bible-reading-plans
One Year: www.TheBible.net/read/sched.pdf
90 Days: www.HavenMinistries.com/
schedule.pdf

ABOUT THE AUTHOR

S. E. Thomas, M.A. has a bachelor's of science education in English Education from John Brown University (JBU) and a master's in philosophy from the University of Idaho. Thomas was raised in Latin America by missionary, church-planting parents. Thomas has extensive Biblical training from JBU and has worked in Christian ministry for nearly thirty years, having served as Sunday school teacher, Bible study leader, home group host and leader, guest speaker, etc. Thomas has also served as an instructor at the Valley School of Ministry and Leadership in Missoula, MT and as MOPS Coordinator for four years in Moscow, Idaho. Thomas is an award-winning, multi-published author.

Please follow S. E. Thomas on Amazon and Facebook (Facebook.com/AuthorSEThomas).

MORE FROM THE DRAMATIC PEN

TheDramaticPen.com
facebook.com/thedramaticpen
@TDPPress

Complex Simplicity:
How Psychology Suggests Atheists are Wrong
about Christianity
Dr. Lucian Gideon Conway III

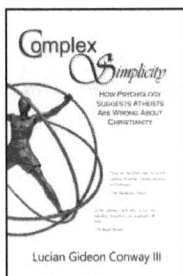

In *Complex Simplicity*, prominent psychology researcher Dr. Lucian Gideon Conway III addresses the modern atheist attack on the psychological effectiveness of the Christian religion. As an expert in the science of cognitive complexity, Dr. Conway uses scientific research and personal narratives to argue that Christianity is an effective guide for reconciling the many complexities built into the human psyche. Directly contradicting what many modern atheists believe, he shows that, in approaching human psychology from a complex perspective, Christianity meets our complex needs with complex solutions. He offers psychological reasons to believe their faith yields positive benefits. To skeptics, he offers a challenge to the growing cultural belief that Christianity is both simple-minded and ineffective.

Daily Life in Bible Times
Small Group Study
S. E. Thomas

Come face to face with the people you read about in Scripture by exploring their daily lives. Learn how a young man selected and courted his bride, what occupations they had and how they trained for them, how infants were cared for, and how the ancients mourned and buried their dead. We will also look at the economic and political climate, learn about crime and punishment, and even find out what they ate and how they dressed. And as you come to know the culture of Jesus Christ, you will see Him more clearly, as well. *This is a 10-week Bible study.* **Workbook & Leader Guide Editions Available.**

Longing for Rest
A Novella
S. E. Thomas

One heartbroken woman battles insomnia. Another cannot escape the coma trapping her between dreams and reality. Though they have never met, through a miraculous crossing of consciousness, they find themselves together on a grassy hill surrounded by a mysterious fog. Will fear, pain, and betrayal follow them and spoil this haven? Will they finally be able to rest? Can a dream change your life? Available in paperback ($7.99) or eBook ($2.99 from Kindle or Nook.)

The Scrolls of the Nevi'im Series:

Book I: Habakkuk's Plea: A Prophet of Elohim
Book II: Habakkuk's Plea: Evil Persists
Book III: Habakkuk's Plea: Elohim Answers
S. E. Thomas

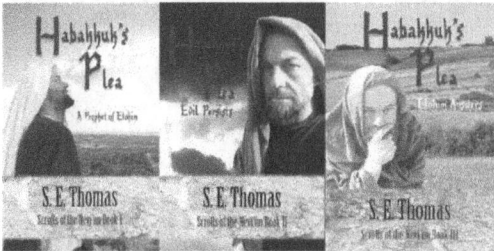

The Sixth Hour
Book I of the Holy Land Mysteries Series
S. E. Thomas

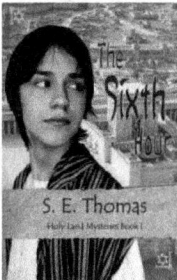

Can Darash, a Jewish teenager, track a killer, rescue his family from ruin, and discover the truth about Yeshua? The rebel, Yeshua, drove the merchants and moneychangers from the Temple with a whip. Hours later, one of them was murdered. Now fifteen-year-old Darash must find a way to protect his family from poverty even as he struggles with the grief of losing his father. When another murder is committed, Darash finds himself searching for a dangerous killer and relying on an old, blind basket-weaver for help. But will he be able to expose the killer before the killer finds him?

**Interactive Mystery Party Games
for Teens and Adults
S. E. Thomas**

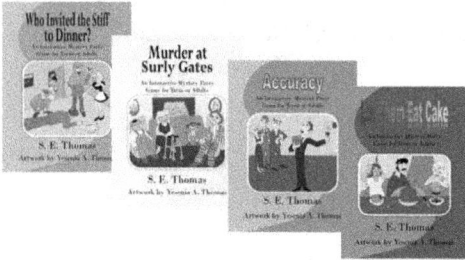

**Who Invited the Stiff to Dinner?
Murder at Surly Gates
Accuracy
Let Them Eat Cake**

**Acting Out Loud
Christian Skits for All Occasions
S. E. Thomas**

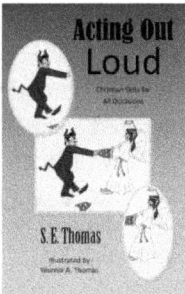

Whether you are a pastor looking for a skit to help drive home your message, a ministry leader desiring a dramatic reading to speak God's love at a retreat or conference, or a youth group leader hoping to spice up a youth meeting, we have the material you're looking for! Find over thirty skits, short plays, and dramatic readings that cover the following areas: Biblical Tales, Christian Living, Evangelism, Special Events, Holidays.

Into the Beautiful
Poetry by Montana Artists Series

"Into the Beautiful: Poetry by Montana Artists" is a series of poetry books by Montana artists of all ages. These works of art and creativity were collected through annual contests run August through October 15th. To find out more about this contest, please visit our website at www.TheDramaticPen.com.

Lazy Dog
carol fields brown

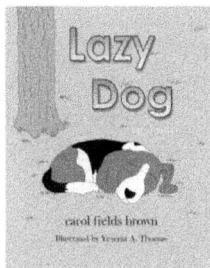

"The quick brown fox jumps over the lazy dog." This sentence contains every letter of the English alphabet at least once. The Lazy Dog and the Fox start us on an animal adventure. You can write the sentences and color the pictures. At the end of the book is a chart to help you make up your own sentences. Every sentence can become a story. This coloring book provides an opportunity for young learners to explore the intricacies of the English language, practice their handwriting, and explore a variety of animal behaviors in a fun and creative way. Full-color illustrations, matching coloring pages, and lines for handwriting practice are also included.

**Sourdough Secrets… Revealed!
From Making the Starter to
Sourdough Success!
Ray Templeton**

Step-by-step instructions that will allow you to make your own starter, make your first loaf, and even learn to make sourdough bread in your bread machine.

Please Visit Us Again!

Find books, study guides, plays, skits, mystery party games, fundraising resources, free downloadable program templates, writers' resources, and much more at:

www.TheDramaticPen.com

Write To Bless The World